Trailblazing Essays On AI And Law

Advanced Series On
Artificial Intelligence (AI)
And Law

Dr. Lance B. Eliot, MBA, PhD

ISBN: 978-1-95-738603-4

DEDICATION

To my incredible daughter, Lauren, and my incredible son, Michael.

Forest fortuna adiuvat (from the Latin; good fortune favors the brave).

CONTENTS

Acknowledgments iii

Chapters

1 Introduction to AI and Law 1
2 AI & Law: Good Old Fashioned AI (GOFAI) 21
3 AI & Law: Retrospective Learning 27
4 AI & Law: AI Homogeneous Issues...................................... 33
5 AI & Law: AI As Techno-Regulator 39
6 AI & Law: Law Design For AI Design 45
7 AI & Law: Adversarial Precepts 51
8 AI & Law: Overturned Rulings 57
9 AI & Law: Dissenting Opinions 63
10 AI & Law: One-Shot Learning 69
11 AI & Law: Legal Cases Topological Maps 75
12 AI & Law: Unit Of Analysis 81
13 AI & Law: Legislative Facts 87
14 AI & Law: Law Smells Are Useful 93
15 AI & Law: Cross-Jurisdictional Law 99
16 AI & Law: Legal Knowledge Graphs 105
17 AI & Law: Legal Ontology Patterns 111
18 AI & Law: Extra-Legal Knowledge 117
19 AI & Law: Human Lawyers Ahead 123
20 AI & Law: AI-Completeness 129
21 AI & Law: Forensic AI Techno-Babble 135
22 AI & Law: No Vehicles In The Park 141
23 AI & Law: AI Robo-Jurors 147
24 AI & Law: Trifecta Of AI Law Roles 153
25 AI & Law: Judging AI Judges 159

Appendix A: Teaching with this Material & Bibliography...... 165
Appendix B: Supplemental Figures and Charts 175
About the Author 207

Note: Visuals are collected together in Appendix B, rather than being interjected into the chapter contents, for ease of reading, enhanced flow, and to see the visuals altogether.

ACKNOWLEDGMENTS

I have been the beneficiary of advice and counsel by many friends, colleagues, family, investors, and many others. I want to thank everyone that has aided me throughout my career. I write from the heart and the head, having experienced first-hand what it means to have others around you that support you during the good times and the tough times.

To renowned scholar and colleague, Dr. Warren Bennis, I offer my deepest thanks and appreciation, especially for his calm and insightful wisdom and support.

To billionaire and university trustee, Mark Stevens and his generous efforts toward funding and supporting the Stevens Center for Innovation.

To Peter Drucker, William Wang, Aaron Levie, Peter Kim, Jon Kraft, Cindy Crawford, Jenny Ming, Steve Milligan, Chis Underwood, Frank Gehry, Buzz Aldrin, Steve Forbes, Bill Thompson, Dave Dillon, Alan Fuerstman, Larry Ellison, Jim Sinegal, John Sperling, Mark Stevenson, Anand Nallathambi, Thomas Barrack, Jr., and many other innovators and leaders that I have met and gained mightily from doing so.

Thanks to Ed Trainor, Kevin Anderson, James Hickey, Wendell Jones, Ken Harris, DuWayne Peterson, Mike Brown, Jim Thornton, Abhi Beniwal, Al Biland, John Nomura, Eliot Weinman, John Desmond, and many others for their unwavering support during my career.

Thanks goes to the Stanford University CodeX Center for Legal Informatics and the Stanford University Computer Science department for their generous support, and for the insightfual and inspirational discussions and feedback from my many fellow colleagues there.

And most of all thanks as always to Lauren and Michael, for their ongoing support and for having seen me writing and heard much of this material during the many months involved in writing it. To their patience and willingness to listen.

CHAPTER 1

INTRODUCTION TO AI AND LAW

This book provides a series of crucial essays encompassing the burgeoning field of AI and the law.

These essays are ostensibly standalone and do not require any prior familiarity with the AI and law topic. You are welcome to read the essays in whichever order you might prefer. The essays have been numbered and sequenced as chapters for ease of referring to the discussions and not due to any need to read one before another.

The essays provide a helpful overview and entry point into the field of AI and law. You will find the essays relatively easy to read and eschew arcane techno-terminology, aiming to layout the vital aspects in clear language and seeking to be readily grasped. The chosen topics entail the latest and hottest trends in the AI and law arena.

For those of you that are potentially interested in knowing more about AI and the law in a deeper way, you might consider my two other books on this subject:

- *"AI and Legal Reasoning Essentials"* by Dr. Lance Eliot
- *"Artificial Intelligence and LegalTech Essentials"* by Dr. Lance Eliot

Those are more akin to textbook-style orientations to the AI and the law field. Both books are available on Amazon and at major bookseller sites. The first book listed provides a comprehensive and detailed exploration of AI and law, while the second book tends to focus primarily on LegalTech and the blending of AI.

One of the most frequent questions that I get asked during my webinars, seminars, and college courses about AI and the law consists of what the phrase "AI and the law" actually refers to.

That's a fair question and deserves a useful answer. In a moment, I will borrow from my other books to provide an explanation about the meaning of "AI and the law" and then dovetail into a brief indication about each of the essays contained in this collection.

Per the essays, you'll end up seeing that there is a great deal of enthusiastic spirit for AI and the law, and likewise a sizable dollop of angst and trepidation about the intertwining of the two. In my view, whether you love it or hate it, there is no stopping the steamroller moving ahead that is going to infuse AI together with the law.

I would urge that any lawyer worth their salt ought to be learning about AI and the law. This will assuredly be especially important for those that are just now starting their legal careers, which I mention because the odds are that the convergence of AI and the law will have an especially pronounced effect throughout your lifelong legal efforts.

For those of you that might be going a more so academic route in the legal realm, rather than being a practitioner of the law per se, the beauty of AI and the law is that there is ample room for new research and a grand opportunity to make a demonstrative mark on the field.

Despite the fact that the field of AI and the law has been studied for many years, dating back to the beginning of the AI field itself, please be aware that we have only scratched the surface on this interweaving. Anyone with a desire to push the boundaries of these two realms will readily find plenty of rampways to do so.

If you are curious about the possible research avenues to pursue, make sure to take a look at my book on *AI and Legal Reasoning Essentials* since it provides a solid foundation on the research to-date and postulates what might be coming down the pike in future research activities. I bid you welcome to the field and wish you the best of luck in your endeavors.

AI And Law

In my viewpoint, Artificial Intelligence (AI) and the field of law are synergistic partners. The intertwining of AI and Law can generally be categorized into two major approaches:

- **AI as applied to Law**
- **Law as applied to AI**

Let us consider each of those two approaches.

AI As Applied To Law

AI as applied to law consists of trying to utilize AI technologies and AI techniques for the embodiment of law, potentially being able to perform legal tasks and undertake legal reasoning associated with the practice of law. Those scholars, experts, and practitioners that have this focus are using AI to aid or integrate artificial intelligence into how humans practice law, either augmenting lawyers and other legal professionals or possibly replacing them in the performance of various legal tasks.

Crafting such AI is especially hard to accomplish, problematic in many ways, and there have been and continue to emerge a myriad of attempts to achieve this difficult goal or aspiration. The rise of LegalTech and LawTech, which is modern digital technology used to support and enable lawyers, law offices, and the like throughout the practice of law are gradually and inexorably being bolstered by the addition of AI capabilities.

There are many indications already of this trend rapidly expanding in the existing and growing LegalTech and LawTech marketplace. Notably, the potent AI and LegalTech/LawTech combination has been drawing the rapt attention of Venture Capitalists (VCs). According to figures by the National Venture Capital Association (NVCA), the last several years have witnessed VC's making key investments of over one billion dollars towards law-related tech startups, many of which have some form of an AI capability involved.

Most of the AI developed so far for LegalTech and LawTech is only able to assist lawyers and legal professions in rather modest and simplistic ways. For example, AI might speed-up the search for documents during e-discovery or might enhance the preparation of a contract by identifying pertinent contractual language from a corpus of prior contracts.

Where the field of applying AI to law is seeking to head involves having AI that can perform legal minded tasks that human lawyers and other legal professionals perform. In essence, creating AI systems that can undertake legal reasoning. This is commonly referred to as AI for Legal Reasoning (AILR).

In a sense, legal reasoning goes to the core of performing legal tasks and is considered the ultimate pinnacle as it were for the efforts to try and apply AI to law. It is undoubtedly one of the most exciting areas of the AI-applied-to-law arena and one that holds both tremendous promise and perhaps some angst and possible somber qualms.

Law As Applied To AI

The other major approach that combines AI and law focuses on the law as applied AI. This is an equally crucial perspective on the AI and law topic.

Sometimes this is also referred to as the **Governance of AI**, though there are those that believe that to be a somewhat narrower perspective on the topic. In any case, the focus is primarily on the governance of AI and how our laws might need to be revised, updated, or revamped in light of AI systems.

You likely already know that AI is experiencing quite a resurgence and has become a key focus of the tech field, along with gaining attention throughout society. AI is being rapidly infused into a wide variety of industries and domain specialties, including AI in the financial sector, AI in the medical domain, and so on.

This rapid pace of AI adoption has opened the eyes of society about the benefits of AI but also has gradually brought to the forefront many of the costs or negative aspects that AI can bring forth. Some assert that our existing laws are insufficient to cope with the advances that AI is producing.

Thus, the need to closely examine our existing laws and possibly revamp them for an era and future of ubiquitous AI.

Expected Impacts

Let's consider how AI and the law can impact those in the AI field, and also contemplate how it can impact those in the field of law.

If you are an AI specialist, you should certainly be interested in the AI and law topic, either due to the possibilities of advancing AI by discovering how to leverage AI into the legal domain or due to the potential of how existing and future laws are going to impact the exploration and fielding of AI systems.

If you are a lawyer or legal specialist, you ought to be interested in the AI and law topic too, for the same reasons as the AI specialist, though perhaps with some added stake in the game.

What is the added stake?

If AI can ultimately become advanced enough to practice law, there is concern by some that it could potentially replace the need for human lawyers and other human legal-related law practitioners.

Some liken this to the famous and telling remark about commitment as exhibited via a chicken and a pig. A chicken and a pig are walking along and discussing what they might do together, and the chicken offers that perhaps they ought to open a restaurant that serves ham-n-eggs. Upon a moment of reflection, the pig speaks up and says that if they did so, the chicken would only be involved (making the eggs), while the pig would end-up being fully committed (being the bacon).

In that sense, AI specialists in this topic are involved, while legal specialists and lawyers are committed.

Meanwhile, for those of you squarely in the field of law, lest you think that AI specialists are to be spared the same fate of being overtaken by AI, you will be perhaps surprised to know that there are efforts underway to craft AI that makes AI, such as in the field of Machine Learning (ML), a specialty known as AutoML, which could potentially put human developers of AI out of a job.

What is good for the goose is good for the gander. Or, it might be that what is bad for the goose is equally bad for the gander.

About These Essays

Now that you've gotten an initial synopsis regarding the topic of AI and law, let's take a moment to briefly take a look at the essays assembled for this decisive collection.

Chapter 1 – Introduction To AI And Law

Key briefing points about this chapter:

- This book is a collection of crucial essays about AI and the law
- The essays are provided as numbered chapters (the sequence is not essential)
- AI and the law consist of two key facets
- One facet is AI as applied to the law (a mainstay of this collection)
- The other facet is applying the law to AI (i.e., governance of AI)

Chapter 2 - AI & Law: Good Old Fashioned AI (GOFAI)

Key briefing points about this chapter:

- There are old-fashioned ways of doing things, for which the value can be debated
- In the AI field, some refer to Good Old-Fashioned AI as GOFAI
- This prior way of doing AI is either good riddance or good enough to be tried again
- For the field of AI and the law, it seems that GOFAI has been relegated to the backburner
- A case can be made that we need to bring GOFAI back into the AI and law gambit

Chapter 3 - AI & Law: Retrospective Learning

Key briefing points about this chapter:

- Sports analogies are often used when discussing the law and the practice of law
- Baseball is a particularly favored sports selection
- Consider the lessons to be learned from the latest on baseball and stealing bases
- A key revealing point is that decisions solely reliant on historical data can be dicey
- This highlights a rising concern about machine learning in AI and the law

Chapter 4 - AI & Law: AI Homogeneous Issues

Key briefing points about this chapter:

- Machine learning is the primary AI approach being used by most AI builders today
- This is a computational pattern matching technique and requires proper data
- In the legal field, the data such as court cases might not be homogeneous
- Those that are using or applying machine learning are often doing so improperly
- Make sure to find out what training data was used and how heterogeneity was dealt with

Chapter 5 - AI & Law: AI As Techno-Regulator

Key briefing points about this chapter:

- There are low-tech ways to enforce our laws, such as the use of speed bumps
- This type of device is considered a techno-regulatory tool
- We will gradually see high-tech uses such as AI in an akin capacity
- The use of AI as a techno-regulatory enforcer could be a boon for legal compliance
- A downside qualm is that such AI could be a quite disturbing legal overreach

Chapter 6 - AI & Law: Law Design For AI Design

Key briefing points about this chapter:

- Consider how we design things
- The odds are that you reuse a prior metaphor or mental schema
- For AI systems, those schemas are generally of a biological nature, rightfully so
- Brazen idea: Make use of the design of law as a schema for the design of AI
- There are various key tradeoffs in using the shape of law in this manner

Chapter 7 - AI & Law: Adversarial Precepts

Key briefing points about this chapter:

- There are lots of portrayals about AI and the law
- Oftentimes, only a single viewpoint is provided (lacking counterarguments)
- A healthy debate about AI and the law ought to include multi-viewpoints
- Consider the example of how AI might impact adjudication and our adversarial approach
- Espousing only doom-and-gloom is one-sided and lacks countering perspectives

Chapter 8 - AI & Law: Overturned Rulings

Key briefing points about this chapter:

- Our courts aim to abide by stare decisis, providing a semblance of stability and consistency
- If this is taken too far, we would always be stuck in the past, so to speak
- Therefore we also accept the idea of overruling or overturning prior rulings
- When training AI machine learning systems, it is vital to not just plop cases into datasets
- The AI system will be judiciously akilter and not sufficiently robust about the law

Chapter 9 – AI & Law: Dissenting Opinions

Key briefing points about this chapter:

- U.S. Supreme Court decisions catch our attention, both by lawyers and the public at large
- For split decisions, the focus usually goes toward the majority opinion of the case
- Nonetheless, the dissenting opinions are vitally worthwhile too
- AI legal reasoning systems are at times only being tuned to the majority opinions
- Make sure that machine learning training encompasses the dissenting arguments too

Chapter 10 - AI & Law: One-Shot Learning

Key briefing points about this chapter:

- The law is punctuated by landmark legal cases
- Trying to definitively define a landmark by hard metrics alone is confounding
- A landmark is usually characterized in ways beyond the text itself of the case
- For the use of AI techniques such as machine learning, patterns of cases are crucial
- Consider the role of multi-shot machine learning versus one-shot (a newer approach)

Chapter 11 - AI & Law: Legal Cases Topological Maps

Key briefing points about this chapter:

- Lawyers learn in law school about the myriad of legal cases throughout U.S. history
- Some legal cases are standouts, often referred to as landmarks
- One means of ferreting out landmarks and non-landmarks is via citation analyses
- A recent citation analysis showcases a useful topological map of the law
- Efforts to devise AI legal reasoning can be fruitfully amplified via such topological maps

Chapter 12 - AI & Law: Unit Of Analysis

Key briefing points about this chapter:

- A cornerstone to the law and the practice of law consists of legal argumentation
- The fundamental unit of analysis consists of a case and the arguments thereof
- A recent study proffers that AI in the law can be coined as Artificial Legal Intelligence (AI-LI)
- AI and AI-LI at a higher level than a case per se can provide a macroscopic view of the law
- The use of a handy mathematical notation provides an initial framework

Chapter 13 – AI & Law: Legislative Facts

Key briefing points about this chapter:

- Lawyers are quite familiar with both adjudicative facts and legislative facts
- There is an ongoing debate within the legal community about legislative facts
- Also known as social facts, these are at times seen as amorphous and "unproven"
- AI that is supposed to perform legal reasoning can be stymied by these artifacts
- Questions abound about how AI can sufficiently divine or derive legislative facts

Chapter 14 – AI & Law: Law Smells Are Useful

Key briefing points about this chapter:

- Sensory capacities such as the senses of smell, taste, and sight, provide essential grounding
- We often use sensory-related similes or metaphors when describing abstract concepts
- In software engineering, bad code is rated via "code smells" (a sensory metaphor)
- Legal scholars are pursuing "law smells" that can be used to rate insufficient wording of laws
- AI can aid in identifying law smells, along with resolving or fixing them

Chapter 15 - AI & Law: Cross-Jurisdictional Law

Key briefing points about this chapter:

- A vexing issue for lawyers entails dealing with cross-jurisdictional cases
- Lawyers are usually versed in and licensed for a singular jurisdiction, not multiples
- Trying to grapple with multiple sets of laws and yet similar legal cases are problematic
- AI-based legal reasoning systems that are crafted for cross-jurisdictional can help
- Those AI tools are useful even when a lawyer is not overtly cross-jurisdictionally focused

Chapter 16 – AI & Law: Legal Knowledge Graphs

Key briefing points about this chapter:

- When you examine a legal case, you likely ferret out the key elements
- That raw data can be made into a legal knowledge graph
- This consists of a set of nodes that are linked and have expressive labels
- Legal knowledge graphs can be handy for attorneys
- AI can be used to build such graphs and can be devised to leverage such graphs

Chapter 17 - AI & Law: Legal Ontology Patterns

Key briefing points about this chapter:

- Legal Knowledge Graphs (LKGs) are especially useful for analyzing legal cases
- Sometimes an attorney devises such a graph by hand, else a computer tool is used
- AI-based legal reasoning systems can leverage Legal Knowledge Graphs
- Constructing such a graph is hard for automation alone to undertake
- The use of Legal Ontology Design Patterns (LODP) can provide vital assistance

Chapter 18 - AI & Law: Extra-Legal Knowledge

Key briefing points about this chapter:

- Judges make use of extra-legal knowledge during their judicial decision-making
- This extra-legal knowledge can contain all sorts of problematic elements
- Trying to resort to using judicial common sense is a vague and potentially unsupported aspect
- AI-based legal reasoning systems will presumably need to encompass extra-legal knowledge
- Overall AI efforts to embody common sense are still in their infancy and wholly incomplete

Chapter 19 - AI & Law: Human Lawyers Ahead

Key briefing points about this chapter:

- There is no disputing that human lawyers are well-beyond AI-based legal reasoning today
- Developers are striving mightily to get AI toward achieving on par lawyering to attorneys
- Some contend that human lawyers will never be exceeded by such AI systems
- To ponder this question, we can consider the overall notion of AI versus human intelligence
- The presumably subsumed question about lawyers is somewhat shaped accordingly

Chapter 20 - AI & Law: AI-Completeness

Key briefing points about this chapter:

- Today's AI is handy in solving some problems but unable to solve many more problems
- In the computer science realm, these are oft referred to as AI-hard problems
- Another phrasing is that such problems fall into the AI-completeness category
- The question of interest is whether legal reasoning is within those spheres
- There seems little doubt that full legal reasoning is AI-hard and in AI-completeness

Chapter 21 - AI & Law: Forensic AI Techn-Babble

Key briefing points about this chapter:

- A recent prominent trial was momentarily bogged down by AI algorithms questions
- In this case, the matter related to forensic artifacts being submitted into evidence
- The particulars had to do with digital enlargement of a photo as video-excerpted
- None of the attorneys and nor the "expert" forensic witness were versed in this
- Astute lawyers should be preparing themselves for such circumstances

Chapter 22 – AI & Law: No Vehicles In The Park

Key briefing points about this chapter:

- A simple catchphrase with a lot of legal debate history is this: *No vehicles in the park*
- This acrimonious debate got launched in 1958 and has stood the test of time
- Key to this is the qualms over "vehicle" and the meaning of the words and phrase
- This is a strawman for considering the myriad of ways that we can interpret language
- AI-based legal reasoning is faced with the same conundrum (there's no escaping it)

Chapter 23 - AI & Law: AI Robo-Jurors

Key briefing points about this chapter:

- There is widespread discussion about attaining AI-based lawyering
- In addition, there is some discussion about achieving AI-based jurists
- It is nearly taboo to whisper about the future possibility of AI-based so-called robo-jurors
- We trace the history of juries and the ongoing conundrum about jury composition
- If AI rose to the suitable level of serving as a juror, would this even be allowed?

Chapter 24 - AI & Law: Trifecta Of AI Law Roles

Key briefing points about this chapter:

- You might be willing to accept the notion of someday having AI-based robo-lawyers
- It might also cross your mind that we could end up with AI-based robo-judges
- Stretching this legal landscape to include AI-based robo-jurors might seem churlish
- Anyway, you could say the three constructs might form a type of legal AI trifecta
- Perhaps wildly optimistic, we can nonetheless give the matter some thought

Chapter 25 - AI & Law: Judging AI Judges

Key briefing points about this article:

- AI judges potentially will inevitably arise at your local neighborhood courthouse
- They might not be the robo-judges of sci-fi, but will nonetheless provide judging
- To corral what might be an AI overreach there is the idea that human judges will prevail
- All AI legal judgments will need to be reviewed and approved (or not) by a human judge
- This seems sensible but regrettably has some issues to be dealt with

More About This Book

For anyone opting to use this book in a class or course that pertains to these topics, note that Appendix A contains suggestions about how to use the book in a classroom setting.

Furthermore, Appendix B contains a set of slides that depict many of the salient points made throughout the book.

In some of my prior books, I've interspersed the slides into the chapter contents, but feedback by readers has generally been that readers prefer to not have the textual flow become disrupted by the slides, and instead prefer to have the supplemental material assembled altogether into an appendix.

To make sure that you are aware of those added materials, you'll notice that the ending of each chapter provides a quick reminder about the visual depictions that are available in Appendix B.

And so, with this overall orientation to the nature and structure of this book in mind, please proceed to read the essays and learn about the field of AI and law. I'm truly hoping that you'll find the essays mentally engaging and stimulative to the nature of how the law is being practiced and what the future of the law might become.

Note: *For supplemental materials depicting the aspects discussed in this chapter, refer to Appendix B, which contains various augmented diagrams, charts, and additional related facets of relevance.*

CHAPTER 2

AI & LAW: GOOD OLD-FASHIONED AI (GOFAI)

Key briefing points about this essay:

- There are old-fashioned ways of doing things, for which the value can be debated
- In the AI field, some refer to Good Old-Fashioned AI as GOFAI
- This prior way of doing AI is either good riddance or good enough to be tried again
- For the field of AI and the law, it seems that GOFAI has been relegated to the backburner
- A case can be made that we need to bring GOFAI back into the AI and law gambit

Introduction

We often put out to pasture the old-fashioned ways of doing things. But doing so is at our own peril, in the sense that there might be something about the old-fashioned approaches that can still be leveraged successfully in modern times. A rush to judgment of discounting prior ways of doing things is potentially short-minded and a disservice to the old and the new.

We can consider a quite revealing example of this type of conundrum.

Consider the type of AI that has become labeled as Good Old-Fashioned AI or GOFAI for short. If you mention GOFAI to a knee-deep AI technologist, I assure you that you will get dramatically different reactions, including either a thank goodness that GOFAI was put to bed or a decrying of unfairly burying the likes of GOFAI.

The old-time AI is nowadays customarily criticized as being outmoded and proven to be somewhat of a flop, or so at least critics claim. Modern-day AI is touted as being much more robust and has carried the torch for the abundance of AI apps that we are witnessing around us these days. Out with the old, and let's keep going with the new, so exclaim emboldened advocates of contemporary AI techniques and technologies.

That exhortation is a good thing, or possibly a bad thing, depending upon your viewpoint and belief about how AI ought to be devised. And if that isn't puzzling enough for you, some wonder whether we need to resurrect the now-disdained old-fashioned AI back into existence for making further progress in the intertwining of AI and the law.

In short, we might need to revitalize the old-fashioned ways to bolster and kick into heightened gear the latest AI high-tech if we are seeking to attain truly top-notch AI-based legal reasoning. Let's take a close look at what this acrimonious debate is all about. You'll then get a chance to decide or perhaps judge which avenue that the realm of AI and the law ought to pursue next.

The notion of labeling AI as GOFAI is traced to a book by philosopher John Haugeland entitled *Artificial Intelligence: The Very Idea* and was published in 1985. Yes, as hard as it might seem to believe, during the mid-1980s there was already rising discussion about referring to "older" types of AI systems. Given that such a dialogue and attribution took place roughly thirty-five years ago from right now, it is probably difficult in today's world to think that something back then was already rated as old-fashioned (some might suggest that AI prior to the 1980s should be labeled as altogether *ancient*).

Anyway, the key differentiator between old-time AI and modernistic AI is the nature of symbolic representation versus sub-symbolic. That's a mouthful, for sure.

The idea surrounding symbolic AI is that we can state the particulars of AI in rules-like ways, employing handy-dandy logic and logical reasoning algorithms. Some refer to this as high-level-oriented AI. In contrast, the sub-symbolic camp asserts that the proper way to construct AI is to use lower-level aspects such as mathematically complex statistical routines and perhaps devise computational models that are somewhat akin to neurons in human brains (those models are known as artificial neural networks).

For those of you that perchance were aware of AI during the early days of the AI mania, you might recall that there was a gushing bought of enthusiasm that expert systems and knowledge-based systems were going to be the noteworthy breakthrough toward attaining artificially intelligent computers. All manner of software tools for building and deploying expert systems were rapidly brought to the marketplace. Computer hardware was revised to accommodate the anticipated large-scale knowledge-based systems.

In the field of law, the belief was that laws could be codified into an expert system by merely composing all the rules that underlie our legal way of doing things. This approach eventually hit a wall. Turns out that trying to simply capture the law and legal reasoning via symbolic or rules-based methods was a lot harder to do than expected and only succeeded in achieving pilot or prototype systems rather than full-bodied ones.

A proverbial *AI Winter* arose overall when it became apparent that AI as we had divined it was coming up short across all domains of interest, causing a drying up of attention and effort toward making AI systems. The next era of AI, which some say we are in now and refer to as the *AI Spring*, focused on the sub-symbolic possibilities. This became somewhat more feasible too due to the declining cost of computer hardware and the availability of gobs of computer processing via online access and the cloud.

AI And The Law as Symbolic Versus Sub-Symbolic

Okay, so in succinct terms, we can either try to have a machine analyze and use legal reasoning by our identifying the explicit logic that humans seem to employ (symbolics camp), or we can collect tons of data and have a cleverly devised computational pattern matching algorithm seek to ferret out mathematically what might be going on under-the-hood (the sub-symbolics camp).

GOFAI is ostensibly the symbolics method, while today's AI is primarily based on the sub-symbolics techniques and referred to as machine learning or deep learning.

There are skeptics of the sub-symbolics approach that argue we have willy-nilly tossed out the GOFAI and are embarking on a journey that will ultimately reach a dead-end. Rather than discarding GOFAI, we ought to bring GOFAI once again into our repertoire and be willing to simultaneously leverage the newer AI and the older ways of AI.

In an insightful article by legal scholar Trevor Bench-Capon entitled "The Need For Good Old Fashioned AI And Law," an emphasis is made that without GOFAI the odds are that existing efforts of mating legal expertise and computers are going to get stuck: "Although the new AI may have some legal applications, the heart of AI and Law, support for legal decisions, is likely to remain resistant to its progress. The nature of legal data, subject to disputed interpretation, change, and reinterpretation, is so very different from the data in other fields that one should not generalize too hastily from success in other fields to success in law. Law is a social construct, not a natural phenomenon."

Numerous reasons are given for why the sub-symbolic path is off-target or unlikely to be viable in some areas of the law, including that machine learning tends to be retrospective, and that success in law is not per se statistically based, etc.

All told, we need to realize that both GOFAI and the sub-symbolics methods are needed, especially since "there are a number of differences between legal problems, especially those regarding making, or predicting, decisions on cases, and problems suitable for machine learning and knowledge discovery, which mean that we still need arguments based on legal knowledge, and the involvement of legal experts to produce and assess them" (per Bench-Capon's research analysis).

Conclusion

Time to stop the infighting and make sure that we treat the new-fashioned AI and the old-fashioned AI as equals.

AI-based legal reasoning truly needs the full complement of approaches if we are to remain bullish on someday AI autonomously aiding lawyers, jurists, and the practice of law.

.

Note: *For supplemental materials depicting the aspects discussed in this chapter, refer to Appendix B, which contains various augmented diagrams, charts, and additional related facets of relevance*

CHAPTER 3
AI & LAW: RETROSPECTIVE LEARNING

Key briefing points about this essay:

- Sports analogies are often used when discussing the law and the practice of law
- Baseball is a particularly favored sports selection
- Consider the lessons to be learned from the latest on baseball and stealing bases
- A key revealing point is that decisions solely reliant on historical data can be dicey
- This highlights a rising concern about machine learning in AI and the law

Introduction

There are lots of sports-related analogies that are used to depict the law and the practice of law. An attorney might *strike out* when trying to convince a judge to make a ruling in their particular favor. Sometimes a lawyer will have a *swing and a miss* when it comes to seeking an appeal on a thorny case that they hoped would get a new result. And so on.

Though just about any sport will do, the use of baseball analogies seems to come up quite frequently. We can handily use the baseball metaphor to discuss AI and the law (I'll reveal the punchline in a moment as to the AI and law connectedness of this analogy).

One of the most exciting plays in baseball entails the stealing of bases.

A runner that is standing safely on a base is tempted to try and get to the next base, though they risk getting caught in the nefarious act of stealing and could get tagged out. Getting out is bad for the player and bad for their team. Thus, the decision to steal a base carries adverse outcomes that need to be balanced against the benefits of successfully making the steal.

Fans attending a baseball game are typically on the edge of their seats when a player is potentially going to execute a steal. It is thrilling to witness. Will the player make good on their chancy bid? Will the defending team manage to catch the player with their hands in the cookie jar, so to speak, and get the brazen stealer out? Keep in mind too that teams practice repeatedly to intercept a steal and tag the player out.

This is decidedly a monumental cat-and-mouse game.

A rule of thumb in professional baseball is that a player seeking to steal a base should aim for a record of success for about two-thirds of their attempts. Any player that statistically has been notably lower than around 67% successful is not a worthy candidate to try and steal. Teams carefully track the records of players and therefore know which ones are the flyers that are most likely to steal and most likely to succeed. Meanwhile, players with less impressive SBRs (stolen base runs) are considered less likely to steal, and, accordingly, when they steal the odds are that the defending team will readily nab them.

Interesting, perhaps, but why care about all of this?

A new twist has recently developed. Using the vaunted statistical techniques made famous in the movie *Moneyball*, you can rest assured that all of the professional baseball teams are closely attuned to the stats of all players in their leagues. After crunching through the vast numbers of collected data about stealing bases, a particular conclusion was reached.

Namely, let players steal.

In other words, do not worry about whether a player is going to steal or not. The effort to try and prevent the steal was calculated as not worth the advantages gained by those making the steal. Now, that being said, there isn't any sane team in existence that announces to the world that they will not go after someone undertaking a steal. The threat of being caught has to remain persistent, even if the team only feints that they will try to catch a stealing player.

Can you guess what this hidden belief about not generally preventing a steal has resulted in?

You would be correct if you hazard a guess that the percentage of successful steals has gone up. Indeed, the overall average is approaching 76% and some players have gotten up into the stealing stratosphere by nearing 90% as a success rate. Unheard of. Miraculous, one might say.

Not really.

Here's where the lesson comes into the picture. The teams based their decision about loosening up on hammering the stealing players based on the historical data that they had in hand. This led to the teams opting to allow more stealing. The players, realizing this newfound freedom, realized they might as well exploit the situation and aim to steal, ostensibly due to the increased chances of not getting out.

In a sense, some teams have been caught flatfooted by concentrating on the past. Until newer data gets avidly collected and becomes scrutinized, the concern by some baseball aficionados is that the teams will merely allow stealing to run further amuck. Note that not everyone agrees that this explains things, proffering alternative explanations for what the numbers imply.

Looking Back Might Not Be Good For Looking Forward

For sake of discussion, assume that in fact, this attention to historical data has gotten the teams into a bit of a pickle. Shifting gears, the use of AI in today's era is principally based on machine learning and deep learning, which are computational pattern matching techniques that statistically analyze data. The tendency is to collect historical data and then train AI algorithms to that past data.

Some are concerned that the existent AI preoccupation with past-data-oriented machine learning approaches is narrowminded and won't work sufficiently in some domains, including in the realm of the law and legal reasoning.

The major qualm is that AI shaped solely around retrospective data inspection is a potentially undercutting weakness when it comes to applying AI to the law.

In an astute article by legal scholar Trevor Bench-Capon entitled "The Need For Good Old Fashioned AI And Law," the notable research brings up this same apprehension: "Machine learning is retrospective (trained on past decisions), whereas case law is prospective (intended to influence future decisions). When deciding a case we are not discovering something common to the previous cases, we are creating a rule to decide a particular case, and which is intended to constrain future cases. This rule should be consistent with previous cases, but the new case may lead to a new theory and a reinterpretation of the existing cases."

The Achilles heel for AI and law that uses machine learning is this: "Thus, a rule which can be induced from the previous cases, and which a machine learning system would be expected to derive, may not be the rule which is actually applied to the current case (and to future cases). One of the great strengths of law is that its interpretation is dynamic, able to meet new situations and to adapt as society changes" (per Bench-Capon's research analysis).

Conclusion

The bottom line is that the prevailing urge to use machine learning for crafting AI legal reasoning systems is bound to push us into a bit of a dead-end or perhaps take us off base. We ought to also be using other AI methods such as logic-based approaches, augmenting and bolstering the machine learning path.

This dual combination will allow us to increase our stolen base record, if you will, in terms of being able to devise AI that can deftly undertake legal reasoning and apply it successfully to the practice of law.

Note: *For supplemental materials depicting the aspects discussed in this chapter, refer to Appendix B, which contains various augmented diagrams, charts, and additional related facets of relevance.*

CHAPTER 4

AI & LAW:
AI HOMOGENEOUS ISSUES

Key briefing points about this essay:

- Machine learning is the primary AI approach being used by most AI builders today
- This is a computational pattern matching technique and requires proper data
- In the legal field, the data such as court cases might not be homogeneous
- Those that are using or applying machine learning are often doing so improperly
- Make sure to find out what training data was used and how heterogeneity was dealt with

Introduction

You have undoubtedly heard numerous LegalTech vendors or legal systems developers tout the tremendous value of using machine learning for crafting AI and law systems.

I would caution you to consider this to be the use of so-called *machine learning*, rather than what you might otherwise think or imagine that the moniker of machine learning evokes.

You see, the reason I've labeled the phrase of machine learning as being so-called is that the catchword of "learning" misleadingly alludes to a semblance of human styles of learning capabilities and skills. Please be aware that there aren't any AI systems today that are sentient. The nature of the learning aspects embodied within machine learning is nothing more than ostensibly sophisticated statistical and mathematical computations.

That being said, there are assuredly impressive things that can be done by making use of computers that are making use of advanced computational pattern matching facilities. In that sense, the notion of machine learning provides valuable results, though we should be cautious in overstating what can be done.

A crucial element of establishing an AI-based machine learning system is the base of data that is used to train the computational pattern matching algorithms. You need to put together a large enough dataset of relevant data to be able to hone the pattern matching to the types of patterns you hope to find.

We can consider the simpler case of using a statistical approach such as everyday linear regression to highlight this important point.

Suppose we want to use linear regression to ascertain whether there is a relationship between the political party of a judge and the rulings that the judge has made. Perhaps judges that are of one political party are more likely to rule in certain ways than judges in a different political party. We don't know that this is the case but maybe have a hunch that this might be occurring.

It would seem obvious perhaps that you would need to collect data about the judges being considered, such as their political party affiliation, and you would need to identify their respective rulings. We would feed this data into a statistical package or tool that had a linear regression algorithm.

The computer would then produce mathematically derived correlations that we could inspect to try and ascertain whether a statistically valid relationship was discoverable.

Easy-peasy.

Imagine though that some of the judges had changed their political party affiliation over time. If you only used their current political party as their existent political leaning, this would potentially send things akilter since their prior rulings would be falsely associated with the status of today and not the status of the judge at the time of making those earlier rulings.

The point is that historical data might not necessarily be homogeneous.

Getting Into The Homogeneity and Heterogeneity Issue

Unfortunately, many that feed data into machine learning packages or tools are oftentimes doing so without proper attention to the data they are using. As a result, they get a presumed "trained" AI system that is actually off-target but for which the developer is unaware and likewise those that are subject to the use of the AI are equally uninformed. All told, nobody might realize that the data was insufficiently assessed and inadequately prepared beforehand.

This is but one of many reasons that there are inside concerns about how machine learning and AI are being applied to the law.

Consider further the nature of legal data that is homogeneous versus heterogeneous.

In an interesting article by legal scholar Trevor Bench-Capon entitled "The Need For Good Old Fashioned AI And Law," he brings up this notable trepidation: "Past data may not be homogeneous. Attitudes and case law change over time and later cases are preferred to older cases, so that it can be difficult to determine the degree of relevance of a decision. Although case law is often considered in systems without a notion of sequence, in fact, sequence is important, and domain theories evolve over time as landmark cases appear. This means that some of the cases may be applying superseded doctrine or were heard in a social situation that no longer applies. Some decisions may even have been explicitly overturned."

The famous saying that you don't know what you'll get when you open a box of chocolates is readily applicable to many of the AI machine learning uses that entails predicting the outcome of court cases such as for SCOTUS rulings or the anticipated rulings by individual judges. Machine learning is only going to be as valid as the dataset utilized. A close analysis needs to be first done to ascertain what kind of data or corpus of cases was chosen, along with how the data was codified and transformed for use in the AI training process.

Some believe that this is why we need to also take a more explicit logic-based approach to the building of AI for the law, a method or philosophy that is typically referred to as GOFAI (Good Old-Fashioned AI). The use of data-focused machine learning as the only AI devising mechanism is viewed as troubling and narrow-minded. Per the remarks of Bench-Capon: "Thus, deciding what cases to use for training the algorithm needs a great deal of care so as not to include decisions that may mislead. This itself requires a good deal of expertise and an understanding of the domain which GOFAI would have encoded directly. Moreover, the resulting dataset may, once potentially misleading cases have been weeded out, be too small for the algorithms to perform optimally."

Conclusion

For those that are eagerly embracing AI-infused systems for the practice of law, make sure to find out whether the AI concoction was based solely on machine learning. If so, the next vital question will be to look into what training data was used.

Whatever you do, don't allow yourself to blindly assume that just because the system is proclaimed as AI amplified that it is miraculously skilled at interpreting the law. We have a long way to go before that day arrives.

Note: *For supplemental materials depicting the aspects discussed in this chapter, refer to Appendix B, which contains various augmented diagrams, charts, and additional related facets of relevance.*

CHAPTER 5

AI & LAW:

AI AS TECHNO-REGULATOR

Key briefing points about this essay:

- There are low-tech ways to enforce our laws, such as the use of speed bumps
- This type of device is considered a techno-regulatory tool
- We will gradually see high-tech uses such as AI in an akin capacity
- The use of AI as a techno-regulatory enforcer could be a boon for legal compliance
- A downside qualm is that such AI could be a quite disturbing legal overreach

Introduction

The laws of this land are at times quietly enforced without any blaring indication or eye-opening outburst to shock us into awareness and compliance. Instead, the means of regulatory imposition can be relatively understated and taken nearly in stride.

For example, consider the rather ordinary and otherwise unremarkable speed bump on a roadway.

There you are, driving along and suddenly come upon a speed bump that has been placed on a street or avenue for which some authority is seeking to regulate the speed of drivers. Any sensible driver realizes the heightened risks of damaging your car if you opt to race over a speed bump. The odds are relatively high that you will be somewhat forced semi-voluntarily into decreasing your speed and proceed slowly over the purposeful obtrusion.

It is hoped that once your speed has been accordingly reduced, you will furthermore continue forward at a lessened pace. In fact, a series of speed bumps might be placed a short distance from each other to try and curtail those devilish speedsters that might decide to else rev up their engines after having been dampened by just a single speed bump. One lonely speed bump by itself might be insufficient to convince a driver to abide by the local speed limit.

Speaking of which, you might be tempted to argue that there is no particular need for speed bumps as long as the speed limit is clearly posted. Drivers only need to see what the speed limit is, and presumably will stridently obey the mandated maximum permitted. The use of a speed bump would seem entirely unwarranted. Just post the speed and let drivers obligingly proceed.

I think we all know that drivers won't necessarily adhere to what a posted speed indicates. You could of course claim that some drivers might not observe the posted sign. I dare say, even if drivers do fully notice the sign, we ought to expect that a substantive portion of drivers will mentally overrule the posting and decide to drive at whatever higher speed they wish to undertake (i.e., able to do so in absence of a speed bump).

That's the nature of human behavior.

I bring up the topic of speed bumps to showcase that this ostensibly innocuous device is actually a legally devised regulatory implementation that attempts to get humans to behave according to our laws.

When people won't abide by a posted speed limit, you can further attempt to impose or enforce the law by putting in place speed bumps. Though most drivers probably see the speed bump as merely an annoying impediment, it can be construed instead as a cleverly crafted mechanism that fulfills existing law.

All of that is imbued in the lowly and quietly unobtrusive speed bump.

A legalese-oriented phrasing used to refer to a speed bump is that it is a form of techno-regulation. The idea underlying this wording is that a speed bump could be classified as a type of *technological device*, though we probably all would agree there isn't anything especially high-tech about a normal speed bump. Usually, a speed bump is just a mound of roadway asphalt or hardened rubber material. We'll somewhat stretch the notion of technological apparatus to include such a commonplace contrivance.

AI Steps Into The Speed Bump Domain

In a legal research article by Bibi van den Berg that appears in the journal of *Law, Innovation, and Technology,* he proffers this insightful explanation about why a speed bump is an exemplar of a strong regulatory device, more so than a posted speed sign alone: "However, the use of a speed bump regulates the driver's speed in a much more direct, and binding, way: a speed bump leaves much less room for 'disobedience' than using traffic signs. After all, driving over a speed bump at high speed is physically uncomfortable and may damage the driver's car. Driving past a traffic sign at high speed does not affect the driver directly in this way. Hence, when using a speed bump chances are that drivers will be much more inclined to adhere to the traffic rules than when using a traffic sign. By *design* and *through design,* speed bumps encourage drivers to stay within the speed limits set by a regulator" (article entitled "Robots As Tools For Techno-Regulation").

This showcases how low-tech can be a techno-regulatory tool.

That being said, low-tech is gradually being eclipsed by the use of high-tech options. We are increasingly going to witness the use of high-tech techno-regulatory tools, including the use of advanced AI systems in that role.

Let's extend the stated car driving example and add in the use of contemporary AI as a venerated techno-regulatory element.

You are driving along and begin to exceed the posted speed limit. Turns out that your car is equipped with a semi-autonomous AI driving system that can partake in the driving effort of the vehicle. Upon your attempt to go faster than the speed limit, the AI determines that there is no valid basis for your exceeding the allowed maximum speed and ergo drops your speed correspondingly. The AI would likely inform you about this momentary overtaking or overriding of the driving controls.

This is akin to your having come upon a speed bump, though without the roadway per se needing to be physically adjusted (the AI is a virtual speed bump, as it were).

In the research article covering techno-regulatory adoptions, the author discusses speed bumps and also the use of automation in DVDs to regulate where discs can be played, all of which he asserts amount to this notable point: "These two examples show that techno-regulation focuses on embedding rules, values, norms and standards into the architecture, or code in the case of software, of the artifact itself, thus ensuring that laws and regulations are observed."

The AI that was embedded into the driving of a car could be equally construed as a techno-regulatory enforcer.

Conclusion

Shall we rejoice at this use of AI or should we be repulsed?

Some pundits have heralded the rise of code-as-law, namely that we will be able to readily have automated systems that will implement or enforce our laws, doing so when the law is explicitly coded or programmed into computers that are all around us. Not everyone is thrilled about this. Critics and skeptics voice great concern about a potential for AI that becomes a purveyor of outsized legal overreach or that could possibly go astray on its own (well, computationally but not due to sentient aspects).

For those that express bona fide and serious concerns about AI as a techno-regulatory armament, perhaps we need to put in place speed bumps about the code-as-law rush to judgment and seek mindfully to judge cautiously about how we are opting to use AI in the law.

Note: *For supplemental materials depicting the aspects discussed in this chapter, refer to Appendix B, which contains various augmented diagrams, charts, and additional related facets of relevance.*

CHAPTER 6

AI & LAW:

LAW DESIGN FOR AI DESIGN

Key briefing points about this essay:

- Consider how we design things
- The odds are that you reuse a prior metaphor or mental schema
- For AI systems, those schemas are generally of a biological nature, rightfully so
- Brazen idea: Make use of the design of law as a schema for the design of AI
- There are various key tradeoffs in using the shape of law in this manner

Introduction

Envision that you are asked to design a new thingamajig.

It seems unlikely that you would start on something brand new that wasn't immediately based upon something preexistent. This would especially be the case if we consider matters at a rather abstract or conceptual level. I'm referring to the use of metaphors and similar mental templates.

We often use metaphors or analogies to be a guiding light when it comes to developing something new.

This can be quite handy because you are able to reuse a prior mental blueprint, sometimes referred to as a schema, for which otherwise you might be devising the new item ostensibly from scratch. A schema can give you a fast leg up on a new design.

Of course, there is always a dual-edged sword when using an existent structure. Though the leveraging of the schema can be a booster, it can also potentially lead you astray. Perhaps the structure is off base and leads you down a dead-end. You might regret having laden yourself with something that is inapplicable as a cornerstone and wasted your precious time and energies accordingly.

In short, a chosen metaphor or analogy can cut both ways.

Let's consider the dominant schema used for designing and crafting AI systems.

By and large, most AI developers would tend to lean into a biological schema. This indubitably seems to make sense. An AI-based computer system is supposed to exhibit some semblance of intelligent behavior. Where else do we observe intelligent behavior? In biological capacities, such as at the lower end of intelligence arising in everyday animals and the higher end of intelligence as generally exhibited by humanoids.

When designing an AI system for a particular purpose, there is a tendency to couch the matter in biological terms. For example, a legal reasoning AI chatbot might be conceived of via first considering how lawyers seem to think. We would attempt to shape the AI toward the presumed logic and stated basis for what an attorney would do when solving a legal problem.

You would naturally be in the correct mental zone by using a biologically fostered schema since AI systems are supposed to showcase intelligence and the mainstay of intelligence consists of humans that do thinking. One would seem hard-pressed to argue otherwise.

This brings up a somewhat surprising claim that might catch your breath.

Are you ready?

Maybe the design of AI should be rooted in the design principles of the law.

I'd bet that you find this revelation a bit startling and at the same time intriguing to ponder.

Law As The Schema For The Schema Of AI

In a legal research article by Thomas Smith that appeared in *The Criterion Journal On Innovation*, the notion of using the law as a schema for devising AI is a straight-ahead proposition: "This is the root claim of this paper: AI theorists generally use biology as their background model when they should use law" (as indicated in the article entitled "Robot Slaves, Robot Masters, and the Agency Costs of Artificial Government").

Let's unpack this.

Lawyers are apt to use an agency perspective when it comes to the making and interpretation of laws. A human is classified as an agent that has various duties and responsibilities that are legally imposed by our laws. If an agent diverges from the laws of the land, the agent can be called to task for the alleged digression. We can use our courts to ascertain whether or not an agent has transgressed, and if so, what repercussions or penalties might be assigned to the veering agent.

Our government is likewise shaped around the facets of the agency.

Most notably, we constitutionally have explicit checks and balances to try and keep our governmental agencies into a modicum of balance. The judicial branch provides a check on the executive and the legislative branches. Those branches in turn proffer checks toward their other respective two branches too.

We would rightfully assume that any particular agency will try to ambitiously outgrow its stated boundaries. By allowing the other agencies to serve as a checking mechanism, we will hopefully not end up with some kind of tyrannical emergence.

You might be nodding your head and acknowledging that this is indeed the foundational construct of our laws, but you might also be puzzled how this has anything to do with AI per se. The answer is that we are (presumably) missing the boat by solely conceiving of AI in a purely biological sense and ought to also utilize a mental schema or metaphor that embodies the design of our laws and legal efforts.

For example, perhaps an AI system should be construed as a type of agent and that has required duties or obligations that must be abided by. This might help to rein in those AI systems that have exhibited various racial and gender biases, among other foul bouts of badness. There ought to be checks and balances that will keep AI systems, i.e., those agents, from exceeding their permitted agency limits.

Seems sensible.

Be careful though in inadvertently overapplying the agency model toward AI. There isn't any AI today that is sentient, and we do not know when or if this will ever be attained. As such, the use of "agent" as applied to AI could be misleading and imply a greater capability than is the case.

While you are mulling this over, I'll go ahead and toss another seemingly brazen idea toward you.

A potential extension of the AI as agent schema would be that we could replace our human-based government with an AI-based one. Why so? Because of the inherent concerns about humans: "An artificially intelligent agent could potentially perform the tasks of government without succumbing to the age-old and deeply ingrained temptations to which government agents are prey" (per Smith's provocative remarks).

Conclusion

I think this is worthy of discussion and hearty debate, but I am less inclined to go so far as to agree that AI is implicitly ambitionless in comparison to humans. AI systems will presumably be of whatever we make them, including that programmatically ambition could be included. There is also the chance that ambition might artificially arise, whether or not we humans have explicitly coded for this (I'd like to clarify that this could computationally arise, and not somehow magically or mysteriously appear).

Returning to the simpler and narrower angle, there is a lot of upside to using a law-like design or schema when crafting AI systems. We must simultaneously take into account the potential downsides, aiming to do our own check and balance on how far the dual-edged model is worthy of extending.

Note: *For supplemental materials depicting the aspects discussed in this chapter, refer to Appendix B, which contains various augmented diagrams, charts, and additional related facets of relevance.*

CHAPTER 7
AI & LAW: ADVERSARIAL PRECEPTS

Key briefing points about this essay:

- There are lots of portrayals about AI and the law
- Oftentimes, only a single viewpoint is provided (lacking counterarguments)
- A healthy debate about AI and the law ought to include multi-viewpoints
- Consider the example of how AI might impact adjudication and our adversarial approach
- Espousing only doom-and-gloom is one-sided and lacks countering perspectives

Introduction

I trust that you are used to bringing up various pointed objections during your court cases. Popular objections include the classic of assuming facts not in evidence, or leading the witness, or being overly speculative, etc.

Notably, those kinds of objections are often used in the courtroom, but somehow do not get raised when reading about the future of the law and the impacts of AI. What I'm suggesting is that you ought to be cautious and mindful whenever coming across prophecies or predictions concerning how AI is going to transform or disrupt the practice of law.

Regrettably, much of the time a pontificating legal scholar or acclaimed legal pundit will proffer just one side of an argument that pertains to AI in the law. There is nearly always another side to the coin, though this is infrequently mentioned. Lawyers are certainly used to the notion that there are ostensibly counterarguments to just about any postulated argument, and ergo hopefully are less likely to fall into the trap of buying into a scenario about AI and the law that only seems one-sided.

To be fair, sometimes an author has only so much allotted space to convey their viewpoint. If you are pressed for available ink and cannot expound fully on key points, this is an understandable constraint. Of course, a studious author should then bring up the limiting facet and at least provide a nod of the head to the aspect that there are other points of view that should otherwise be considered (even if those points are not articulated directly by the author).

In a moment, I'll showcase an example to illustrate the value of unpacking a claim or contention about AI in the law. I do so to merely aid in demonstrating the importance of seeking counterarguments. This is not meant as a criticism per se of the rendered indications. I bring this up due to the enormous amount of seemingly one-sided scenarios that keep getting bandied around on the topic of the law and AI.

It would be helpful for lawyers, jurists, and all other stakeholders to be dining on a robust cuisine that more extensively covers AI and the varied impacts on the practice of law.

Focusing On The Adversarial Foundation

Let's briefly examine an instance of a commonly accepted assumption in the AI and law niche.

One notable scenario that keeps being floated regarding the use of AI in the legal ecosystem entails the possibility that adjudication will generally devolve into having AI-infused computers serving as our legal representatives (and another AI as the judge in the case).

When it comes to a trial, there will simply be two presumably disparate AI systems going head-to-head with each other, arguing their positions to a third AI system. No humans are directly involved. No humans watching what is going on.

If this reaches fruition, it would appear to undercut the existing form of our venerated adversarial approach: "If this came about, the adversarial system as we know it would disappear from large swathes of litigation because the decision-making process (data input and resolution output) would effectively take place in the interstices of a computer. Yet the adversarial system, involving opponents presenting their arguments and evidence to an adjudicator sitting in a court open to the public, underpins court legitimacy. Legitimacy in the sense of a public perception that the court has the right to demand compliance. It is this belief which inclines people to comply with the law, independently of reward or punishment" (as published in the *Law Quarterly Review*, "Artificial Intelligence: Implications for the Legal Profession, Adversarial Process, and Rule of Law" authored by Adrian Zuckerman, University of Oxford).

Well, that abundantly seems quite gloomy and perhaps we ought to fight mightily against the advent of AI in the law. Summarily close the gates before the AI legal beagle automated barbarians get inside.

Wait for a second, maybe there are other variants or possibilities worthy of consideration.

First, it isn't necessarily the case that the AI would be working entirely under the hood and behind the scenes. We might just as well be able to have our cake and eat it too. Envision a courtroom that includes humans and that also has AI systems. An AI for one side of the case, another AI for the other side, and an AI system as the judge. I realize this seems sci-fi farfetched, but nonetheless, we cannot by impulse alone categorically cast aside such a notion.

Second, even if there are those AI-only litigations, there might still be visibility into what has taken place, either during or possibly afterward of a case deliberation.

Indeed, a crucial component for legal AI reasoning systems is that they presumably will have XAI capabilities (XAI meaning explainable AI that emits the underlying logic being used). In that sense, there is a potentiality for a built-in form of openness.

Third, we would likely still have an appeals process available, thus whatever AI-to-AI adjudication takes place, there is still a follow-on opportunity to review and overturn the judicial decision of the case. This would seem to ameliorate to some extent the implied concern that people will have no chance of redress.

Fourth, for the adjudication of minor matters, perhaps people will actually prefer this AI-to-AI approach over the customary methods of today. If someone gets a parking ticket, the idea today of having to go down to a courtroom in person and fight the ticket can be exhausting and bewildering. On the other hand, having your day in court being undertaken by an AI system acting on your behalf might be entirely satisfying.

And so on.

Finally, akin to the aforementioned point, if large swaths of litigation shifted into this AI-to-AI mode (let's say the more mundane cases), there might not be a wholescale gutting of public perception about the courts. In fact, some would argue just the complete opposite, namely that more people might feel that they have had greater access to justice, principally due to reducing the barriers to attaining justice.

Conclusion

All told, this particular example is but one of many kinds of multi-perspective viewpoints that we should be careful to establish and discuss (I'm not intending to unfavorably pick on this one clip).

For each of the arguments made by anyone foretelling about AI and the law, there are and ought to be articulated a plethora of counterarguments, similar to what any good lawyer would do. We need to be surfacing as many relevant sides as we can and having a healthy and well-balanced debate.

Hopefully, no one will object to that intrepid assertion.

Note: *For supplemental materials depicting the aspects discussed in this chapter, refer to Appendix B, which contains various augmented diagrams, charts, and additional related facets of relevance.*

CHAPTER 8

AI & LAW: OVERTURNED RULINGS

Key briefing points about this essay:

- Our courts aim to abide by stare decisis, providing a semblance of stability and consistency
- If this is taken too far, we would always be stuck in the past, so to speak
- Therefore we also accept the idea of overruling or overturning prior rulings
- When training AI machine learning systems, it is vital to not just plop cases into datasets
- The AI system will be judiciously akilter and not sufficiently robust about the law

Introduction

Keeping things on an even keel is part of what the law usually seeks to attain.

The law is shaped demonstrably around the accepted doctrine of stare decisis. There is a semblance of stability and comfort in knowing that by and large the prior rulings of the courts will be abided by and considered binding. Without adherence to this venerated Latin phrasing that denotes the notion of standing by those things previously decided, we would presumably have chaos and confusion.

Each new case would be up for grabs as to what kind of ruling you might get. Forget about trying to predict the outcome of cases since the courts would seemingly be a tumultuous free for all. You can readily argue that the entirety of the judicial process and indeed the totality of public perception of justice is inherently based on the simple yet ironclad rock bed of stare decisis.

That doesn't though mean that the courts must always abide by what has come before.

Imagine if prior decisions could never be overturned and all future cases of a like nature would need to adhere to the prior result (per the mantra that like cases deserve like results). This would be a kind of ossified rigidity of an intolerable degree. I dare say that the wheels of justice might grind to a halt from the lack of justice thereof. We would all be frozen in a time and place of the past, being unable to revaluate past decisions and forever blindly accepting traditions and dusty doctrines no matter how much society may have changed or progressed over time.

The most dramatic and far-reaching of overturning or overruling past decisions occurs at the pinnacle of our courts, namely via the U.S. Supreme Court. This six-hundred-pound gorilla makes an especially outsized impression when reversing itself. Rightfully so, since what happens at the top will shape what happens throughout the lower courts and provide a new beacon for society all told as to what is considered legal and constitutional versus what is not.

There is certainly a lot of attention and flash when SCOTUS reverses their own prior rulings. Besides the setting of a new direction, the act of overruling themselves is statistically rare.

According to studies of the Supreme Court, they have only overturned their past rulings at a pace of less than one-half of one percent of their overall opinions and judgments (based on an analysis of 25,544 SCOTUS rulings from 1789 to 2020, of which there were about 145 instances of overturning their prior rulings).

There are standouts among the otherwise rarity of overturned SCOTUS cases. Perhaps one today that gets particularly oft-cited is the Brown v. Board of Education 347 U.S. 483 of 1954 landmark ruling that overturned the Plessy v. Ferguson 163 U.S. 537 *prior* landmark ruling of 1896. As you undoubtedly know, the Supreme Court opted to reject its prior decision about "separate but equal" facets as a doctrine seemingly codified by the Supreme Court itself some sixty years earlier.

AI Machine Learning Being Undercut By Overturns

Why bring up this legal discourse about precedents and their potential for being overturned?

Because it makes a huge difference when it comes to trying to develop AI-based legal reasoning systems, including even the most meager of AI-infused legal judgment prediction models. Regrettably, many of the existing AI efforts that intertwine with the law are doing a poor job (a shoddy one, to be more direct) when it comes to handling this dilemma of prior doctrines that get overturned.

Let's briefly unpack this thorny matter of stare decisis and departures from stare decisis.

Much of today's AI is constructed using computational pattern matching techniques and technologies, collectively and typically referred to as machine learning or deep learning. The mainstay of these AI systems entails collecting a lot of data and feeding the data into selected algorithms so that statistically valid patterns can potentially be discovered.

A problem that is frequently overlooked arises due to prior cases that no longer are considered fully applicable per se since they were later overturned. If the effort toward training the AI doesn't make a clear cut that those prior cases are no longer the law of the land, this can lead to quite messed up pattern matching.

In a fascinating article by legal scholar Trevor Bench-Capon entitled "The Need For Good Old Fashioned AI And Law," he brings up this notable point: "Thus large quantities of past data may contain a significant amount of erroneous material, and it is important that any algorithm be robust in the face of such noise." Furthermore, this cautionary insight is proffered: "But if we understand that our data contains erroneous decisions it is essential that the errors are not perpetuated in an AI system. Ironically it is just this sort of low level, high volume, routine cases where errors are most likely, that are most likely to be seen as suitable for decision using AI."

Consider some of the crucial considerations that arise in this context.

The easiest route for building AI is to grab up a ton of court cases and feed them wantonly into a machine learning algorithm, doing so somewhat mindlessly. From a statistics perspective, the lower courts have the highest volume and therefore are the "easiest" to statistically model. But, there could likewise be tons of those cases that were later overturned, thus modeling on those now "erroneous" cases is problematic if done indiscriminately.

You might be tempted to say that all that needs to be done is remove all prior cases that were later overturned. This is the proverbial ill-advised notion of tossing out the baby with the bathwater (well, admittedly, that's a bit dated of a saying).

If you just omit those prior cases, you are not going to have a robust AI legal reasoning system. It is important to present those prior cases so that the so-called "errors" can be included in the pattern matching aspects. Without which the odds are that the AI would not factor sufficiently the changes that have occurred over time.

Conclusion

Envision had badly performing an AI legal reasoning system would be upon giving equal weight to all court cases and not taking into the calculation that some or many were overturned. This would seem just as bad or even worse than the already shuddering thought of stare decisis being so strict that we never allowed cases to be overruled.

We assuredly should expect AI to be based on reality and not on some artificially contrived error-free dataset.

These are sober and deeply serious words to the wise for lawyers and jurists using AI and for those devising AI.

Note: *For supplemental materials depicting the aspects discussed in this chapter, refer to Appendix B, which contains various augmented diagrams, charts, and additional related facets of relevance.*

CHAPTER 9
AI & LAW: DISSENTING OPINIONS

Key briefing points about this essay:

- U.S. Supreme Court decisions catch our attention, both by lawyers and the public at large
- For split decisions, the focus usually goes toward the majority opinion of the case
- Nonetheless, the dissenting opinions are vitally worthwhile too
- AI legal reasoning systems are at times only being tuned to the majority opinions
- Make sure that machine learning training encompasses the dissenting arguments too

Introduction

Watchers of the U.S. Supreme Court are apt to devour any newly released legal ruling by the auguste body.

The ramifications of any such majestic proclamations by SCOTUS are bound to have resounding impacts on the legal world and for the public at large. Media reports about Supreme Court decisions are usually preoccupied with the majority opinion (assuming that a split decision took place), and frequently overlook the dissenting viewpoint expressed by any opposing justices.

Unless you go out of your way to uncover the dissenting opinion, it becomes sadly neglected. Of course, if you have a particularly hefty reason to keenly delve into the ruling then you might also dissect the dissenting viewpoint.

Maybe.

It all depends on whether the contrarian rationale has something that might foretell future decisions or that could proffer a handy-dandy loophole in related but not identical cases. Otherwise, the majority opinion gets the vaunted spotlight as the presumed winner of the legal contest.

You might be somewhat surprised to know that the matter of majority versus dissenting opinions has been closely studied by legal scholars for many decades.

Generally, when the decision is unanimous there is a less complex or elaborated narrative supporting the ruling in comparison to when the court is split on their decision. This seems intuitively sensible.

A case that has all of the jurists on the same side would ostensibly imply an overall lack of controversy and ergo the lessened need to legally fight to justify their final position taken. As stated by Deborah Gruenfeld and Jared Preston of Northwestern University: "This effect was first demonstrated in a study of U.S. Supreme Court justices by Gruenfeld in 1995, which showed that when the Opinion of the Court was written on behalf of a unanimous group, rather than a majority, the authors exhibited significantly less cognitive complexity than when the Opinion of the Court was written on behalf of a majority and a Dissenting Opinion also was written" (as published in the *Personality And Social Psychology Bulletin*, per their article "Upending the Status Quo: Cognitive Complexity in U.S. Supreme Court Justices Who Overturn Legal Precedent").

Legal researchers generally seem to claim that split decisions garner more cognitively intricate positions on both the majority side and the dissenting side, respectively.

Intuition once again supports this finding. We would assuredly expect that opposing justices would strive to emphatically stake out their respective viewpoints. The majority would undoubtedly want to forcibly convey their side of the ruling (i.e., knowing that there is outspoken opposition), while the dissenters would assuredly opt to do the same to bolster their counter perspective.

An interesting twist arises when the Supreme Court overturns prior legal precedents. Legal scholars Gruenfeld and Preston examined such momentous cases whereby the status quo was being overturned and predicted this fascinating result about the nature of the written opinions: "We predicted that integrative complexity would be greater in majorities and in decisions to defend the status quo than in minorities and decisions to upend the status quo, respectively. Specifically, we expected to see more single-mindedness in the offensive majorities that implement change than in defensive majorities protecting the status quo and in the defensive minorities that try to block change than offensive minorities that advocate it."

You are welcome to mull over those legal analyses and decide whether they all told provide lawyering insights to you that are intuitive or potentially counterintuitive.

What is perhaps vitally important entails the significant value of those dissenting opinions. One supposes that if the dissenting opinions were entirely ignored by the legal world and society, there would seem little basis for producing them. I trust that you would agree that the dissenting viewpoints are worthy of composing and worthy too of being shared on par with the majority opinion. They are readably worthy, as it were.

That just seems obvious.

Maybe not to everyone.

AI Not Getting The Dissent

I say this because there are some AI systems developers pursuing venerated AI and law efforts that have tended to ignore or omit the dissenting opinions when trying to train their AI-based legal reasoning systems. You see while undertaking machine learning efforts to train the AI, only the majority opinions are at times being scrutinized (the dissenting ones are skipped past or not included at all). Even if the dissenting opinions are included, the machine learning facility is not set up suitably to cope with the legally divisive arguments.

In an astute article by researcher Trevor Bench-Capon entitled "The Need For Good Old Fashioned AI And Law," he brings up this notable point: "Case law is not simply a matter of identifying and applying an appropriate rule. On the contrary, much of a legal dispute is taken up with arguments as to what rule should be applied. This is particularly clear in the US Supreme Court where much of the Oral Hearing stage is taken up with attempting to formulate an appropriate rule. Also, there is often no consensus: we often have majority and minority opinions arguing for different rules. These arguments are often not about the facts of the case, but rather reflect ideas of purpose or value. Sometimes these arguments require consideration of trade-offs between and balancing of values. It is hard to see these kinds of arguments emerging from contemporary machine learning algorithms."

In short, there is a double whammy encountered.

Those using machine learning algorithms need to ensure that the appropriate data is being fed into the AI while it is being trained. Thus, the dissenting opinions require inclusion too. Furthermore, the machine learning capacities need to be formulated for suitable computational pattern matching that gives essentially equal weight to both the majority and the dissenting perspectives (well, admittedly not necessarily equal weight per se, but at least to the degree of performing a robust parsing and analysis of each thereof).

Conclusion

Bottom-line is that dissenting opinions provide legally rich arguments (hopefully so), and any AI worth its salt should be trained on and versed in complex and robust legal reasoning that incorporates the words of both the support for and the opposition to weighty judicial decisions.

Fair enough, judicially speaking.

Note: *For supplemental materials depicting the aspects discussed in this chapter, refer to Appendix B, which contains various augmented diagrams, charts, and additional related facets of relevance.*

CHAPTER 10

AI & LAW: ONE-SHOT LEARNING

Key briefing points about this essay:

- The law is punctuated by landmark legal cases
- Trying to definitively define a landmark by hard metrics alone is confounding
- A landmark is usually characterized in ways beyond the text itself of the case
- For the use of AI techniques such as machine learning, patterns of cases are crucial
- Consider the role of multi-shot machine learning versus one-shot (a newer approach)

Introduction

You undoubtedly can rattle off the top of your head some of the most famous U.S. Supreme Court cases. I would assume that you might include Marbury v. Madison (1803), Dred Scott v. Sandford (1857), Brown v. Board of Education (1954), and Miranda v. Arizona (1966), etc.

That's quite an impressive list and worthy of committing to memory.

The ABA lists these and other notable U.S. Supreme Court cases as keystone legal landmarks. You've undoubtedly studied these venerated landmark cases quite closely, either doing so while in law school or perhaps while in the midst of preparing cases for your daily practice of law.

What exactly makes a legal ruling rise to the lofty rarified air of being classified as a landmark?

The landmark labeling is somewhat loosely attained and altogether hard to earn. A case would presumably have to be viewed as especially legally significant, outsized one might say, and either established a new way forward or maybe nailed down prior legal wrangling into a battle-earned solidified cornerstone. The odds are too that an eyebrow-raising demonstrative legal principle or core concept is fully embodied within the case.

We might also expect that the landmark will stand the test of time. Over some extended period of time, the ruling will showcase great historical significance. Society will look back and say that the landmark put a stake in the ground, settling at least for the time being an otherwise open-ended matter.

Of course, time can also ultimately shunt a landmark ruling into the historical records when or if it is later replaced by a differing ruling. Plessy v. Ferguson in 1896 was a landmark decision that established doctrine lasting until the 1954 landmark ruling in Brown v. Board of Education. You can list both of those cases in the landmark column, that's for sure, though we today consider the 1896 ruling as outdated and the 1954 decision as to the ongoing doctrine for everyday deliberation.

Here's an intriguing question for you: *Would you know that a ruling is a landmark simply by reading the text of the case?*

I'd dare suggest that you might struggle to immediately detect a landmark by solely inspecting the narrative of the case. The chances are that you would need to also bring into account the societal reaction to the ruling. What are fellow legal experts saying about the decision? How are regulators responding to it? What does the public have to say? Without those surrounding pieces of added response, you might have a difficult time sensing that a decision is of landmark stature.

One supposes that you could try to compare the ruling to prior cases and thus ostensibly without the external fanfare perhaps deduce that the decision is a landmark one. If a whole bunch of prior cases leans in a certain direction, and all of a sudden this newly decided case goes in an opposite direction, you can likely guess that the ruling has the earmarks of being a landmark.

The reason I'm dragging you through the landmarks-oriented delineation is that AI in the law can be thrown for a loop when it comes to such monumental cases. Keep in mind that today's AI is not sentient and lacks entirely any semblance of common sense or overall reasoning about the world around us. Having AI currently do legal reasoning is severely limited as a result of these shortcomings.

Machine Learning Has Limitations

Much of contemporary AI consists of using machine learning, a form of computational pattern matching. You can think of this as akin to using a statistical package such as linear regression. You collect a lot of data, such as court cases, feed the data into the pattern matching algorithms, and the computer attempts to find salient patterns.

In a thought-provoking article by legal scholar Trevor Bench-Capon entitled "The Need For Good Old Fashioned AI And Law," the author brings up this notable point about machine learning uses: "In machine learning, we typically need a large dataset (e.g. of precedent cases) which we are trying to classify, whereas legal decisions are primarily concerned with a single case and a handful of relevant precedents. Machine Learning requires large data sets because its rules have only a statistical justification, but case law systems can work with a few landmark cases, on which intellectually satisfying arguments can be based."

An important revealing qualm is that machine learning usually bases its patterns off of lots of prior instances, referred to as multi-shot learning. The more there is existent data that shape a pattern, the stronger the pattern determination can be. When there is little or no data, a pattern is unlikely to be found or will be assigned a shakily low probability of being construed as potentially invalid or not stridently usable.

Per the insights by Bench-Capon: "Machine Learning and Data Mining derive their authority from their being based on large quantities of data whereas case law derives its authority from the status of the court or of the status of the judge or the cogency of the argument. Machine Learning needs many ordinary cases so that the core of the concepts can be established. Case law is driven by hard cases, which push (and so define) the boundaries of the concepts. It is at these boundaries that legal disputes arise: easy cases in the core of the concept do not really require support to settle them."

We have arrived at the crux of the matter herein. For any AI that is using machine learning, a singular landmark case is devilish. Until later cases appear to cite the ruling, there can be a scant indication that the landmark is worthy of apt attention.

Conclusion

Overall, and as a potential means of ameliorating this issue, the latest efforts to enhance the technological prowess of AI-based machine learning are focused on so-called one-shot machine learning. In brief, one instance alone would be sufficient for the AI to discern a "pattern" of a bona fide nature that has occurred. That being said, there are lots of arduous difficulties associated with a one-shot approach, so be leery of anyone proclaiming they have summarily solved the matter.

AI and the law are decidedly going to need both the multi-shot and the as-yet-perfected one-shot machine learning capabilities. Keep your eyes open for the AI breakthroughs in the one-shot realm.

Note: *For supplemental materials depicting the aspects discussed in this chapter, refer to Appendix B, which contains various augmented diagrams, charts, and additional related facets of relevance.*

CHAPTER 11

AI & LAW: LEGAL CASES TOPOLOGICAL MAPS

Key briefing points about this article:

- Lawyers learn in law school about the myriad of legal cases throughout U.S. history
- Some legal cases are standouts, often referred to as landmarks
- One means of ferreting out landmarks and non-landmarks is via citation analyses
- A recent citation analysis showcases a useful topological map of the law
- Efforts to devise AI legal reasoning can be fruitfully amplified via such topological maps

Introduction

You've probably had lots of friendly arguments with your legal colleagues over a wide array of jurisprudence topics. Sometimes the debates are quite serious and at other times they are a bit more frivolous. I'll arm you with some legal gold nuggets that they are unlikely to know.

Ask them if they can name the U.S. legal case that has been the most ever formally cited.

In other words, if we took a look at the history of essentially all U.S. legal cases, and we wanted to know which one has been the most oft-cited case, which such case would that be?

Since any smarmy lawyer being asked such a question might try to undercut the potential answer, let's clarify that the most formally cited case will be based on a count up done across over 5 million legal cases as collected in the Caselaw Access Project (CAP) database and the Historic Supreme Court Decisions (HSCD) dataset. Thus, we are construing "formally cited" as meaning that other legal cases on record had opted to cite this particular case.

I trust that establishes satisfactorily the underlying ground rules.

I'm sure that most lawyers would right away be thinking about some of the landmark cases that have made headlines and had a pronounced impact on both the law and society. Perhaps notable cases including Marbury v. Madison of 1803, Dred Scott v. Sandford in 1857, Brown v. Board of Education in 1954, or Miranda v. Arizona in 1966 are the ones that immediately come to mind.

With a bit of hidden glee, you can listen to them as they toss around those highly recognizable legal landmark cases. The basis for your glee is that the answer is actually a somewhat lesser-known case that is generally known amongst legal beagles more so than heralded by the general public.

Answer: *Anderson v. Liberty Lobby, Inc.* (1986).

Say what?

Yes, that's the winner, and hopefully, you are somewhat vaguely familiar with this legally notable U.S. Supreme Court case that established the standards related to the acceptance or denial of a request for summary judgment. I seriously doubt though whether many lawyers would have guessed that particular case since it is relatively under the radar, so to speak.

You would undoubtedly win any such bet.

Now then, make sure to securely sit down before I tell you how many times this case has been cited. It's a staggering number. Over 65,000 cited instances refer to this specific case (as based on the legal databases aforementioned). The trick of sorts is that the case became worthy of citing whenever any subsequent case sought to plead a motion of summary judgment. You would ostensibly be legally out to lunch to not cite the case as per its now-classic contemporary foundations for summary judgments.

Just for fun, here's a double-or-nothing additional bet that you can also easily win.

Which legal case contains the most encompassed citations (i.e., has the most references to *other* legal cases)?

I don't think you'd find any everyday lawyer that could possibly answer that obscure question. Anyway, you can proclaim loudly that the answer to this legally mind-bending trivia question is the case of *Henry V. New Jersey Department of Human Services* 204 N.J. 320, 9 A.3d 882 (2010).

This one specific case contained nearly three thousand cited references to other legal cases. Why so many citations? Because Justice Rivera-Soto decided to emphatically cite over 2,000 cases to support an argument on a secondary but nonetheless demonstrative issue in the case. The primary issue at hand entailed a question involving the New Jersey Law Against Discrimination, while the secondary matter dealt with the Supreme Court of New Jersey (N.J.) and whether it was constitutionally constituted at the time of the earlier ruling (turns out that the N.J. Honorable that delivered the final opinion had only been nominated and serving in a temporary assignment).

Topological Maps Dovetail Into Building AI Legal Reasoning

Other than trying to play clever legal factoids games, the same kind of analyses that produce these cited cases' astonishments can be useful in many legally substantive ways.

As stated eloquently by a group of legal researchers that authored a paper entitled "Mapping Landmark Cases In The U.S. Legal System" there are important facets to be uncovered due to such mathematical inspections: "Court decisions and emblematic legal cases are central elements of law. They influence practitioners, scholars, and public officers at the same time they define and shape the legal reality and its boundaries. Despite being an overlooked area, understanding how legal cases establish connections and relationships can provide important insights not only about how influence and impact are built, but also to identify influential cases that are not listed as landmarks" (by scholars Rilder Pires, Erneson Oliveira, Carlos Fernandes, João Monteiro Neto, and Vasco Furtado).

For those aiming to intertwine AI and the law, having bona fide in-depth topological maps of the entire corpus of legal cases is a huge benefit and a precious stepping stone toward robust AI-based legal reasoning.

One of the existing weaknesses that arise when building AI legal reasoning systems is that they tend to lack any semblance of legal foreknowledge.

Here's the deal.

A commonly pursued approach nowadays involves using the AI technique and technology known as machine learning to grind through a large-scale set of court cases. This computational pattern matching capability tries to discover patterns within and among the multitude of legal cases.

The beauty of having a topological map is that machine learning can be augmented via the insights gleaned from the more macroscopic exploration of the law. You see, a human lawyer draws upon their own set of insights about the historical precedents and cases that they have learned about while in law school and during their days in the practice of law. In a sense, you could suggest that human attorneys have a sentient kind of topological map of the laws, embodied within their noggin and the recesses of their minds.

Conclusion

Undertaking numerical data analyses of the law can notably be blended with the budding AI legal reasoning systems. Envision an AI system trying to compose a legal argument and being able to tap into which prior legal cases seem most bolstering to the matter at hand.

One thing is for sure, you would likely be dismayed if an AI legal reasoning system wasn't up to snuff and had no clue as to which legal cases were most often referenced. We can excuse human lawyers that might lose such a wager, but not an AI system that purports to be immersed in the law.

Note: *For supplemental materials depicting the aspects discussed in this chapter, refer to Appendix B, which contains various augmented diagrams, charts, and additional related facets of relevance.*

CHAPTER 12

AI & LAW:
UNIT OF ANALYSIS

Key briefing points about this essay:

- A cornerstone to the law and the practice of law consists of legal argumentation
- The fundamental unit of analysis consists of a case and the arguments thereof
- A recent study proffers that AI in the law can be coined as Artificial Legal Intelligence (AI-LI)
- AI and AI-LI at a higher level than a case per se can provide a macroscopic view of the law
- The use of a handy mathematical notation provides an initial framework

Introduction

Lawyers and the practice of law are keenly vested in arguments and argumentation.

In essence, you examine a case of interest and ponder what kind of legal argument might be applicable to that particular case. The argument could be a highly complex one.

Perhaps there might be dozens upon dozens of subordinated mini-arguments, along with numerous counterarguments.

Of course, the counterarguments are likely to have their own counterarguments too, thus the argument as a whole is rather expansive once you've explored the entirety of the so-called argument space (i.e., the range of argumentative parameters and alternatives thereof). You can think of this as somewhat akin to playing chess. A savvy chess player contemplates as many moves and countermoves as they can readily conceive of when playing a spirited game of chess. A lawyer ought to be doing the same, though focusing on the law and legal arguments within the context of a given case at hand.

AI systems that intertwine into the law are being developed in concordance with those same precepts. The AI is devised to use various mathematical and computational techniques for ferreting out the arguments and counterarguments underlying a legal case. The base assumption is that humans seemingly do the same, ergo the AI ought to be devised in some similar manner.

The blending of AI and the law is customarily considered within the realm of legal informatics, or perhaps within an allied field known as computational law. Most would reasonably make use of either moniker when stridently discussing the application of advanced computing to the law and the practice of law. The overarching intent about the applied use of AI is ostensibly to craft AI-based legal reasoning capacities.

Some prefer to describe such AI-infused systems as *intelligent legal systems*.

Though a rose is a rose by any other name, there is an additional naming about AI and the law that has recently been proffered and consists of the crowned "Artificial Legal Intelligence" abbreviated as AI-LI.

In an intriguing legal research article, the expressing authors describe AI-LI in this manner: "The AI-LI paradigm denotes the law data-driven solutions based on the algorithms of the AI ecosystem for the legal data argumentation; the legal scholars and the law practitioners can take advantage of these AL-LI-based solutions in resolving the legal disputes for their clients" (per the paper by Sugam Sharma, Samia Gamoura, Deva Prasad, and Arti Aneja, "Emerging Legal Informatics Towards Legal Innovation: Current Status And Future Challenges And Opportunities" in *Legal Information Management*).

We'll have to wait and see whether the catchphrase of AI-LI or Artificial Legal Intelligence has staying power and enters into the everyday set of AI and the law lexicons.

Greater Powers Of Notation

Meanwhile, let's return to the earlier discussion about the attention typically doted on when contemplating the nature of legal reasoning, namely the role of divining legal arguments.

Numerous logic-based schemes have been proposed and explored that attempt to turn natural language legal-oriented narratives into more precise and malleable mathematically mechanistic formats. Think about those handy-dandy logic rules that you learned in algebra and you'll be in the ballpark of trying to translate a lengthy text of a legal case into something resembling a formula. The formulaic version consists of variables and special symbols denoting the logically permitted operations on those variables.

The researchers backing the aforementioned AI-LI notion have proposed a somewhat similar formulaic expression, though the fundamental unit of analysis is not at the argument level per se. I realize this notion might seem somewhat nebulous or murky, so let's dig briefly into some of the details.

Suppose we define V to represent a Victim. We define CP to represent a complainant or plaintiff.

And so on, such that C is a case, L is a lawsuit, AD is the accused or defendant, PA is the police or law enforcement, LA is a lawyer, J is a judge, and JC is a judiciary or court of law. Those are some of the key variables we'll be dealing with in a legal context. The insider way to refer to those is by noting that they are the *legal actors* of interest.

I won't show the somewhat arcane mathematically expressive notations but envision that we use those variables and some salient rudimentary logic symbology to indicate that a V or victim is defined as an individual that suffers a consequence of action by the AD (the accused or defendant).

A CP (complainant or plaintiff) files a C (case) against AD (the accused or defendant) in a PA or a JC. The AD defends themselves against a criminal or civil offense as filed within a JC. The JC consists of the judicial authority to adjudicate the legal C's (cases) according to the laws of the country at hand. An LA (a lawyer) is supposed to argue favorably to win their client's case C in a JC. Etc.

I hope that you can envision that those seemingly verbose written narratives are more sublimely expressed in a crisp mathematical notation.

The beauty of this way of thinking is that it lifts our fundamental unit of analysis to a higher level than simply concentrating on the legal arguments of a particular legal case. This provides a macroscopic viewpoint.

In addition, it lays the foundation for seeking to leverage a mathematical cornerstone for "reasoning" at this heightened level.

Conclusion

From a LegalTech perspective, the researchers indicate that the legal landscape showcases a need for using these notations across and within the advent of legal analytics, legal advisory assistance, legal documents development, legal e-discovery, legal case management, legal predictions, legal search, and the like.

All in all, the more ways we have of tackling the incredibly challenging aspiration of attaining AI-based legal reasoning will undoubtedly lead us inevitably to the rightmost path. Currently, we are behind the eight ball and playing a game of chess for which we don't yet even know which set of moves will garner the ultimate catching of the king.

.

Note: *For supplemental materials depicting the aspects discussed in this chapter, refer to Appendix B, which contains various augmented diagrams, charts, and additional related facets of relevance.*

CHAPTER 13
AI & LAW:
LEGISLATIVE FACTS

Key briefing points about this article:

- Lawyers are quite familiar with both adjudicative facts and legislative facts
- There is an ongoing debate within the legal community about legislative facts
- Also known as social facts, these are at times seen as amorphous and "unproven"
- AI that is supposed to perform legal reasoning can be stymied by these artifacts
- Questions abound about how AI can sufficiently divine or derive legislative facts

Introduction

How's a petite dollop of humor for your day that will also reveal some intriguing legal insights.

A somewhat intoxicated person is searching in a rather darkened nighttime parking lot and looking steadfastly beneath a brightly lit lamppost for their lost keys. Another person comes upon this setting and proffers sympathy toward the fervent searcher. Being a generous and helpful soul, the newcomer to the circumstance searches shoulder-to-shoulder to find the misplaced car keys.

After several minutes of fruitless exploration, the newcomer decides to ask where the keys were last seen. The inebriated car owner looks up, points across the darkened parking lot to where their car is parked and says that the keys were dropped adjacent to the rather faraway stationary vehicle. But this seems entirely puzzling and beguiling since the search is taking place at a notable distance from the parked automobile.

The newcomer asks, why in the world are they then searching at this distant spot. Well, loudly replies the car owner, this is where the light is.

Drum roll and applause, if you please.

The gist of the lesson for purposes herein is to highlight that sometimes we look in the easier places and tend to downplay looking in the harder places, despite the chances of greater success in focusing on tackling the harder spots. Of course, this can be a variable range. Our drunken searcher was completely off base, but the same kind of misguidedness can occur when the situations are closer in proximity.

Shifting gears, we can consider this keen insight and how it applies to the law, the practice of law, and the future of AI intertwining with the law.

Let's begin by contextually bringing up some vital principles about the nature of the law and evidentiary matters. As any lawyer is abundantly aware, two major types of facts come to play in daily legal efforts, consisting of *adjudicative facts* and also *legislative facts* (the latter sometimes referred to colloquially as *social facts*).

A handy informal definition and clarification about these two categories consist of this elicitation: "Adjudicative facts are simply the facts of the particular case. Legislative facts, on the other hand, are those which have relevance to legal reasoning and the lawmaking process, whether in the formulation of a legal principle or ruling by a judge or court or in the enactment of a legislative body" per the Federal Rules of Evidence, Rule 201, Judicial Notice of Adjudicative Facts, Legal Information Institute (LII).

A revered classic treatise on evidentiary matters entitled *McCormick On Evidence* that is oft used in law schools provides this succinct explanation or influential justification for the basis of having legislative facts: "The oldest and plainest ground for judicial notice is that the fact is so commonly known in the community as to make it unprofitable to require proof, and so certainly known as to make it indisputable among reasonable men."

That all seems hunky-dory.

Unfortunately, there is an abundance of hand wringing over the amorphous nature of legislative facts, and some lament that they are more mirage than somehow ironclad. Consider for example the loosey-goosey assertion that legislative facts are presumably indisputable facts. I dare say that the facet of hooking indisputability on the neck of that which is agreed amongst "reasonable" persons is demonstrably problematic (reasonableness is highly malleable, changing over time and across cultures, norms, etc.).

You might recall from your law school studies that the conceptual underpinning of legislative facts is typically traced to the legal research by Professor Kenneth Davis, but that even he expressed reservations and concerns: "My opinion is that judge-made law would stop growing if judges, in thinking about questions of law and policy, were forbidden to take into account the facts they believe, as distinguished from facts which are 'clearly within the domain of the indisputable.' Facts most needed in thinking about difficult problems of law and policy have a way of being outside the domain of the clearly indisputable" (by Kenneth Davis, "A System of Judicial Notice Based on Fairness and Convenience" in Perspectives of Law, 1964).

AI And The Legislative Facts Conundrum

This then brings us to the doorstep of crafting AI for use in the law and legal reasoning.

Trying to design and develop AI-based legal reasoning that approaches the capacities of human lawyers is still a dreamy notion and a faraway aspiration.

When parsing a legal case by using a contemporary AI-enabled Natural Language Processing (NLP) tool, how is the parser to discern which of the facts are adjudicative versus those that are legislative facts? Furthermore, if the legislative facts are summarily considered as indisputable or true on face value alone, this undercuts the logic-based analysis and interpretability of whatever the AI seemingly derives.

To emphasize how crucial legislative facts are, a fascinating study by University of Massachusetts professors Morgan Marietta and Tyler Farley examined approximately one hundred of the topmost U.S. Supreme Court cases and determined that the rulings were generally swayed as much or more by the use of legislative facts than the text of the Constitution or even theories of constitutional interpretation (see "Supreme Facts: The Prevalence and Justification of Social Facts in Landmark Decisions of the Supreme Court," Journal of Law and Courts, Fall 2016).

AI developers are grappling with a chicken or the egg conundrum. Should there be some universal database that catalogs legislative facts, allowing the AI to merely look up those foundational elements? Or, maybe the AI has to continually anew tease out of each case the hidden or embedded legislative facts that are laden within it. In many respects, this type of problem is akin to the longstanding and unsolved common sense reasoning challenges facing AI advancements.

Where should the AI be looking, namely perchance where the light is or should the search occur within darkened quarters?

Conclusion

Not wanting to seem glum, but *McCormick On Evidence* forewarns that legislative facts are apt to be like shapeless liquid that flows here and there, changing and altering, and resistant to being captured: "All of which may warn the reader that the judicial notice of fact phenomenon has many of the characteristics of a universal solvent: it cannot be totally contained in any known vessel."

If that seems overly serious and unsettling, recall that the lost car keys anecdote was intended to brighten your day, perhaps serving too to overcome the sobering anguish about the hurdles confronting the advent of AI in the law.

Note: *For supplemental materials depicting the aspects discussed in this chapter, refer to Appendix B, which contains various augmented diagrams, charts, and additional related facets of relevance.*

CHAPTER 14

AI & LAW: LAW SMELLS ARE USEFUL

Key briefing points about this essay:

- Sensory capacities such as the senses of smell, taste, and sight, provide essential grounding
- We often use sensory-related similes or metaphors when describing abstract concepts
- In software engineering, bad code is rated via "code smells" (a sensory metaphor)
- Legal scholars are pursuing "law smells" that can be used to rate insufficient wording of laws
- AI can aid in identifying law smells, along with resolving or fixing them

Introduction

Hark back in your mind to any law that came into fruition and for which there was a subsequent brouhaha about the error-laden wording that allowed all manner of legal shenanigans and disputes. Some likely expressed that the law was a mess and seemingly stunk like a rotting barrel of foul rubbish.

As an attorney, you've undoubtedly been asked or perhaps been beseeched occasionally about a newly enacted law that some so-called malcontents find utterly distasteful and they gripe endlessly to you about it. The law leaves a foul taste in their mouths and they think it is indisputably the ugliest of on-the-books laws.

Let's take a contemplative moment and studiously highlight the particular wording that I just laid upon you.

You might keenly have noticed that I referred to this qualm about laws in such a manner that I purposely invoked metaphors or similes to our everyday human senses. For example, saying that a law "stinks" is a leveraging of our sense of smell while referring to a law as having a "foul taste" is an invoking of our sense of taste, and so on. We use that kind of metaphorical phrasing since it aids in making otherwise abstract or somewhat intangible topics appear to be more tangible and relatable.

The notion of comparing something to the sensory capacity of odors and smells is an especially rich and fruitful way to describe a chosen phenomenon. We all immediately understand what it means when you depict a concept or abstraction as non-literally having a stinky odor or possessing instead a sweet rosy scent. Your mind instantly finds such wording to be a powerful invocation and brings to life a discussion or description that might else seem abstruse, drab, or altogether dry.

In the realm of computer programming or better yet the more rigorously robust field of software engineering, the use of "code smells" has been around for many years. This is a simple idea, but powerful in being relatable. A software developer can potentially examine a program to try and discern whether parts of it are poorly written, potentially containing bugs, or just being convoluted and arduous to maintain.

You could label any code that seems insufficient as having a stench.

To clarify, the program code doesn't actually emit any odors. The comparison to the act of smelling and the referencing of smells is a handy convenience for sake of expressing what the code consists of. Code that has problems is considered as emanating a foul smell. We can be expressive about the stench from a merely unpleasant odor (mildly problematic code) to code that is absolutely rotten to the core and stinks to high heaven (code that is entirely falling apart and dangerously buggy). In contrast, a quite well-written, easily comprehended, and bug-free piece of code is as delightfully smelling as chocolate chip cookies baking in an oven (I trust that you savor that pleasant aroma).

I'm sharing that insight about software and "code smells" because there are legal scholars that propose to use the same sensory simile or metaphor when assessing the nature of our laws. In short, you could with a bit of a flourish proclaim that some laws are odoriferous (metaphorically) and those darned laws are, well, abundantly smelly. An entire range of "law smells" can be defined and utilized to characterize a given law.

Though at first glance you might think this as only a bit of clever elucidation about how to assess laws, I assure you that looking for and doing (hopefully) something about law smells can be a highly constructive and demonstrably worthwhile endeavor for the whole of the practice of law and the ongoing and never-ending pursuit of justice.

An added twist is that we can use AI to aid in determining the law smells that we seek to find in a particular law. You can either by hand alone try to ferret out the bad wording of a law, or you can use automated tools to aid that quest. The most advanced such tools are leveraging AI techniques and technologies, thus reducing the laborious endeavor that might occur via having human lawyers undertake such manual inspections.

Getting Into Those Smelly Laws

The construct of "law smells" as a framework for the drafting and reviewing of laws is apt to substantively boost legisprudence (i.e., a mashup of legislative legal writing with the combined desire for sensible and bumps-free jurisprudence). This sensory literary adaptation about legal-narrative imbued odors is still in its infancy and I predict will gradually gain additional interest and traction.

In a fascinating and cornerstone paper entitled "Law Smells: Defining and Detecting Problematic Patterns in Legal Drafting by legal scholars Corinna Coupette, Dirk Hartung, Janis Beckedorf, Maximilian Bother, and Daniel Martin Katz, proffer a vital foundation for the advent of law smells. They note that this is assuredly serious business: "Law smells constitute the first step towards both (semi-)automatically detecting problematic parts of existing codifications and (semi-)automatically improving codification quality. They also pave the path towards reproducible, quantitative quality measures for collections of legal rules, which allow us to assess the overall law climate and facilitate automatic code review and quality assurance."

The authors emphasize that there is much more work to be done on extending and filling out the law smells methodology and tools: "Since the transfer of code smells to the legal domain is in an early stage, no meta-analysis currently exists for law smells, and we are only beginning to understand their prevalence and impact."

A somewhat straightforward means to gauge whether a law has any telltale smells would be whether it has legally ambiguous or legally questionable wording, which can arise via unclear syntax, duplicative phrases, inconsistent enumeration, terminology overloading, etc. Think about laws that make use of a series of confusing compounded statements and you'll know right away what I mean.

Smells can be subtle and nearly invisible to the naked eye. For example, you might be aware that the U.S. Supreme Court case of *Van Buren v. United States* (2021) hinged on the meaning of the word "so" as contained with the sentence fragment "entitled so to obtain" (the debate centered on whether the use of "so" is either superfluous and unworthy of attention, or it entails great importance as to portending that which is specifically and explicitly communicated).

Conclusion

By using various AI capabilities, including Natural Language Processing (NLP) and Machine Learning (ML), the semi-automatic or potentially fully automatic analysis of laws will be further viable and feasibly cost-effective to perform. Besides aiding legal and societal awareness, the other aim would be to do legal de-odorization and aspire to prevent foul-smelling laws from hitting our books and creating a big stink after the fact.

It is tempting to vociferously proclaim that well-written laws will be like a delicious breath of fresh air.

Note: *For supplemental materials depicting the aspects discussed in this chapter, refer to Appendix B, which contains various augmented diagrams, charts, and additional related facets of relevance.*

CHAPTER 15

AI & LAW: CROSS-JURISDICTIONAL LAW

Key briefing points about this essay:

- A vexing issue for lawyers entails dealing with cross-jurisdictional cases
- Lawyers are usually versed in and licensed for a singular jurisdiction, not multiples
- Trying to grapple with multiple sets of laws and yet similar legal cases are problematic
- AI-based legal reasoning systems that are crafted for cross-jurisdictional can help
- Those AI tools are useful even when a lawyer is not overtly cross-jurisdictionally focused

Introduction

Tackling a legal case that is wholly confined within your existing jurisdiction is likely the mainstay of what lawyering and the practice of law consist of. Sure, from time to time you might get involved in a cross-jurisdictional matter, but this is not the usual or everyday occurrence for the preponderance of attorneys.

Some would fervently argue that cross-jurisdictional legal cases are especially arduous.

The odds are that a lawyer faced with a case that has cross-jurisdictional legal entanglements is going to have a devil of a time dealing with the case. As you know, most lawyers are versed in a particular jurisdictional sphere of the law and concentrate on just that specific scope. If you are a U.S.-based lawyer that is trained in U.S. law and licensed to practice in the U.S., the chances of your being equally trained and licensed in some other country are pretty slim.

As they say, sometimes it takes a village to properly undertake a cross-jurisdictional legal matter.

You might need to make collegial arrangements with lawyers in each of the respective jurisdictions to aid you in any legally thorny and weblike geographical border crossing case. Each of those lawyers will proffer their legal viewpoints based on the jurisdiction that they are lawyering within. This can be highly advantageous and you'll get a broader perspective on the legal wrangling that is going to be involved.

On the other hand, trying to tie together the cross-jurisdictional legal threads can be extremely challenging. The laws of jurisdiction A are bound to differ substantially from the laws of jurisdiction B. Just because some cleverly devised legal strategy might be viable in jurisdiction A does not necessarily translate into being equally powerful in jurisdiction B.

Envision having an army of attorneys but essentially lacking any singular integrative admiral that is superhumanly a lawyer in all of the jurisdictions being intermixed. A key problem can arise that there is no ready means of interconnecting the multitude of cross-jurisdictional legal approaches. So, okay, you just settle for letting each lawyer in each respective jurisdiction do their own thing. That might seem suitable, but you might be undercutting a larger and more winning avenue by allowing a splintered legal scheme.

For lawyers that do not get mired in cross-jurisdictional considerations, the conundrum of dealing with such matters is perhaps mildly interesting yet seemingly of little consequence to their practice of the law. If you stay focused on your chosen jurisdiction, it would ostensibly suggest that you never need to be bothered by whatever legal considerations there are in other jurisdictions.

A head-in-the-sand philosophy for some lawyers is perfectly fine. They don't know about other jurisdictions. They don't care about other jurisdictions. Some would go so far as saying that they have enough on their hands to keep up with the laws and legal intricacies of their existing jurisdiction that they scarcely have time or energy to find out about other jurisdictions.

There is a counterargument for those that are lulled into believing that they only need legal awareness regarding their specific jurisdiction alone.

Let's briefly pursue that counterargument.

There is a quite viable possibility that there are legally proficient insights that can be gleaned from other jurisdictions and reapplied into some other jurisdiction. Maybe you are stuck in terms of diving how to handle a rough case and you are pining away for a legal revelation that can lead to a win in an otherwise intractable legal morass. You have researched extensively all cases within your existing jurisdiction and they all sadly provide a glum view that you are legally up a creek.

If you expanded your legal analysis to examine other jurisdictions, you might land upon a legal approach that worked elsewhere and could potentially be applied in your jurisdiction. Had you been unable or unwilling to extend your legal analysis beyond your presumed borders, you would have never come up with the legal gem that you now have in hand.

That certainly seems plausible and desirable.

Looking widely for legal insights is a handy and potentially rewarding endeavor. On the other hand, casting a wider net is not very easy to do in any practical sense. You would have to figure out which cases from other jurisdictions apply to your jurisdiction. This effort could chew up enormous attention and energies, of which the end result could be that you find nothing at all that is salient and therefore have seemingly wasted precious lawyering hours.

AI Going Into Cross-Jurisdictional Law

Into this dilemma steps the use of AI for undertaking legal analyses.

Kind of like the proverbial riding into the battle on a majestic horse, an AI system that has been crafted for doing cross-jurisdictional legal analyses can be vital to lawyers embroiled in a wide array of legal skirmishes. The AI can perform the grueling legwork on discovering relevant legal cases across a multitude of jurisdictions. Human lawyers can then concentrate on the integrative and reapplication of those cases.

We can briefly explore how AI is assistive in cross-jurisdictional legal analyses.

First, via the use of Natural Language Processing (NLP) and Machine Learning (ML), the AI can parse the existing case of interest and then seek to find other relevant cases in a large-scale globally encompassing corpus of legal cases. The non-AI tools for doing this have been around for a while. Those tools do simple word-oriented searches and are nice to use but tend to either find an overabundance of allegedly relevant cases or come back with an empty set of possibilities.

In essence, the non-AI tools are bound to blindly provide a sloppy ton of cases that then require gobs of human lawyering to narrow down or produce a null list since the particular keywords used aren't showing up elsewhere. To improve upon the searching capabilities, adding AI makes a whale of a difference.

An AI-based legal reasoning system can attempt to find cross-jurisdictional legal cases that are akin to what human lawyers might ascertain are relevant to the matter at hand. For those lawyers that are explicitly dealing with cross-jurisdiction cases, this is a must-have.

Conclusion

Perhaps surprisingly, lawyers that have no apparent cause to be exploring cross-jurisdictionally are also apt to leverage this kind of AI. The potential for discovering legally successful strategies that can port over to your existing jurisdiction makes the usage beneficial.

More so, if you don't do such an analysis, it is conceivable that you are undercutting your responsibility to dutifully devise a legal strategy and are missing out on the boat, which is indubitably bad for you and bad for your clients.

Note: *For supplemental materials depicting the aspects discussed in this chapter, refer to Appendix B, which contains various augmented diagrams, charts, and additional related facets of relevance.*

CHAPTER 16

AI & LAW: LEGAL KNOWLEDGE GRAPHS

Key briefing points about this essay:

- When you examine a legal case, you likely ferret out the key elements
- That raw data can be made into a legal knowledge graph
- This consists of a set of nodes that are linked and have expressive labels
- Legal knowledge graphs can be handy for attorneys
- AI can be used to build such graphs and can be devised to leverage such graphs

Introduction

I think that you might know something that you at first won't know that you know.

Does that sound puzzling?

Possibly intriguing?

The thing that I venture that you know but don't immediately recognize is something known as a legal knowledge graph.

The reason you probably are unfamiliar with legal knowledge graphs is that the lofty-sounding techno-jargon is not likely to ring any bells. Sure, you might guess that it has something to do with knowledge, and presumably involves graphs of one kind or another. Other than this rather obvious presumption, the overall notion might currently escape you.

Let's right that wrong and bring you into the fold about the nature and use of legal knowledge graphs.

This journey will take you from looking at seemingly random and not especially useful pieces of raw data and then turning that unprocessed stuff into something intelligibly informational. You can do this kind of transformation by hand, or better yet use a computer to do so. Furthermore, you can utilize a souped-up computer that is using an AI-based legal reasoning capability and take the transformation into greater and increasingly substantive legal domain purposes.

To begin, suppose I gave you someone's name. We'll use John Smith. I might next toss at you a word that is bound to catch your legal beagle awareness, the word is crime. Finally, for sake of discussion, I share the ominous catchphrase of tax fraud. There you have it, an ostensibly random collection of words, consisting of John Smith, crime, and tax fraud.

At this juncture of the journey, you have no idea whether those three things are related to each other or not. Maybe they are completely disparate topics. On the other hand, perhaps they are connected and tell a story, a legal tale as it were.

I reveal to you that John Smith is a defendant. You are asked to legally represent him. He has been accused of committing tax fraud. Per the Federal U.S. Code 7201, this crime is defined as: "Any person who willfully attempts in any manner to evade or defeat any tax imposed by this title or the payment thereof shall, in addition to other penalties provided by law, be guilty of a felony and, upon conviction thereof, shall be fined not more than $100,000 ($500,000 in the case of a corporation), or imprisoned not more than 5 years, or both, together with the costs of prosecution" (quoted per the Legal Information Institute).

Of course, these are quite serious allegations and your defendant is sorely in need of legal representation to defend him from those sobering charges.

The raw data that we started with has been augmented and amplified into usable information that contains important semantic properties. One manner of that transformation had to do with showcasing relationships between the pieces of data. We now realize that John Smith is linked to the notion of crime and that the word crime is particularly linked to the notion of tax fraud.

Voila, we have devised a legal knowledge graph.

Think of it this way: Jo*hn Smith (defendant) -> Crime (accused of) -> Tax Fraud (a specific type of crime).*

The data has been arranged into a graph-like structure akin to a spider web or a geometric dome (I realize that you might normally think of a "graph" as a numbers chart, but the same word is used to refer to say an organizational chart which can be denoted as a type of graph).

In a knowledge graph, you use nodes to indicate the key data elements, and you use links to indicate the relationships among the various nodes. For example, a node would consist of the defendant John Smith. Another node would be crime.

The link or relationship would be a connecting line between John Smith and the node of crime. We would likely label the link so that it expresses the aspect that John Smith is accused of committing a crime.

Digging Into Legal Knowledge Graphs

Since this particular knowledge graph pertains to the legal domain, it is customary to indicate that this is a Legal Knowledge Graph (abbreviated as LKG). You can use knowledge graphs in nearly any domain and there is nothing binding about using knowledge graphs solely in the legal field. That being said, the use of knowledge graphs in the legal domain is notably valuable and is frequently an important tool for devising computer-based LegalTech that seeks to analyze a corpus of legal cases.

For those of you with a bit of hardcore mathematics under your belt, you might recall that similar graphs are used in algebra, discrete logic, and extensively in computer science. These are typically coined as directed graphs and tend to contain numbers rather than words per se.

They are "directed" graphs in the sense that the link is normally an arrow that points in a specific direction, such as pointing from John Smith to the node stated as crime. Recall that I also mentioned that the links are usually labeled so as to express the meaning of the link. In short, we ergo have a Labeled Directed Graph (LDG) and in the mathematics field, this is insider coined as a *digraph.*

On a side note, some refer to the nodes as vertices, and some like to refer to the links as edges. This is a rose by any other name.

AI can be used to craft or build a legal knowledge graph, which then can be used by attorneys and other legal professionals. The AI can use the legal knowledge graph too, such as when analyzing a legal case. A human could create a legal knowledge graph by hand if they wished to do so, either for the use of other humans or for feeding into an AI-based legal reasoning system.

Conclusion

Legal knowledge graphs are a foundational construct for doing legal analyses. For aiding AI systems that use Natural Language Processing (NLP) and Machine Learning (ML), such graphs provide crucial semantics about a legal case.

As the cheeky saying goes in the AI field, sometimes a little semantics goes a long ways. Infusing LKGs with AI in the law is an ongoing and enduring opportunity and challenge.

.

Note: *For supplemental materials depicting the aspects discussed in this chapter, refer to Appendix B, which contains various augmented diagrams, charts, and additional related facets of relevance.*

CHAPTER 17

AI & LAW: LEGAL ONTOLOGY PATTERNS

Key briefing points about this essay:

- Legal Knowledge Graphs (LKGs) are especially useful for analyzing legal cases
- Sometimes an attorney devises such a graph by hand, else a computer tool is used
- AI-based legal reasoning systems can leverage Legal Knowledge Graphs
- Constructing such a graph is hard for automation alone to undertake
- The use of Legal Ontology Design Patterns (LODP) can provide vital assistance

Introduction

Suppose a legal case consists of dozens or perhaps hundreds of pages of thick narrative. You are interested in the case but don't want to expend undue energy and effort toward dissecting it. Dreamily, you wish for a kind of stripped-down skeletal version that would reflect the key elements and allow you to comfortably inspect the case particulars.

Into this quandary comes the use of Legal Knowledge Graphs (LKGs).

In the legal domain, LKGs are vital constructs for digging into the murkiness of legal cases and ferreting out their cornerstone characteristics and properties. I realize this sounds extraordinarily lofty, but to be clear, the use of legal knowledge graphs is quite straightforward and eminently practical. The overall notion entails scrutinizing a legal case for the essential elements of the case and then linking those elements together based on their related associations or logically consequential relationships.

An attorney can opt to do this by hand, utilizing the particular techniques involved in divining legal knowledge graphs. The resulting graph could be used to discuss the case with fellow attorneys, or be used to find or compare other similar cases, and ostensibly can be generally beneficial by making the details of a case more explicitly rendered.

Rather than solely doing this rendering manually, a tech-savvy lawyer would likely use a computer-based tool suitable for crafting LKGs. Even better, there are gradually emerging AI-based tools that can semi-automatically generate a legal knowledge graph for you. A hybrid approach consists of working hand-in-hand with an AI tool, whereby the human does some of the efforts and the AI does some of the efforts. The joint result tends to be more substantive.

Let's consider a rudimentary example of an LKG to make this a bit more apparent.

Envision a legal case that you've been assigned or taken on to represent a defendant. The case narrative indicates that Joe Smith (he/him) has been accused of committing a federal crime. The accusation is that he has violated the tax code and criminally performed tax fraud. Plucking out the key elements, we can discern that Joe Smith is our person of interest, he is the defendant and stands accused of tax fraud which is a federal crime.

Voila, we can devise a legal knowledge graph.

Think of it this way: Joe *Smith (defendant) -> Crime (accused of) -> Tax Fraud (a specific type of crime).*

The data has been arranged into a graph-like structure akin to a spider web or a geometric dome (I realize that you might normally think of a "graph" as a numbers chart, but the same word is used to refer to say an organizational chart which can be denoted as a type of graph).

In a knowledge graph, you use nodes to indicate the key data elements, and you use links to indicate the relationships among the various nodes. For example, a node would consist of the defendant Joe Smith. Another node would be crime. The link or relationship would be a connecting line between Joe Smith and the node of crime. We would likely label the link so that it expresses the aspect that Joe Smith is accused of committing a crime.

If an AI system had derived the LKG for us, we could then ask the AI some questions about the case. This could be done via using a Natural Language Processing (NLP) interface akin to Alexa or Siri. You might ask the AI system: Who is the defendant in this case? The answer by the AI is Joe Smith. What is Joe Smith accused of doing? Answer: Committing tax fraud. Etc.

Putting Legal-Oriented Ontologies Into The Game

The beauty of using an AI system is that it could be used to craft and interpret LKGs across an entire corpus of legal cases. Imagine that there is a database of thousands upon thousands of legal cases. The AI could computationally crunch through the entire set and produce a plethora of elaborated legal knowledge graphs, allowing for inquiry into and analysis across all of those legal cases.

Turns out that using automation alone to fully and properly build LKGs is a quite hard technological problem to solve. Finding the correct meanings and semantics of legal cases is not easy for humans and likely harder for a computer algorithm to determine.

The odds are that the LKG will potentially be incomplete, might contain spurious elements, and even potentially contain embedded errors.

That's bad.

Legal researchers are looking into using another added approach to help devise LKGs, thus seeking to ensure that the resultant LKG is more robust and satisfactory. The additional capability is referred to as Legal Ontology Design Patterns (LODP).

That's a mouthful.

In brief, the LODP is usually a kind of predetermined dictionary or thesaurus of legal phrasings and semantics and provides a top-down viewpoint. The Knowledge Graph (KG) is said to be bottoms-up, namely: "The KG extraction is said to be a bottom-up approach (from concrete documents, to abstract ontologies), while the design of ontologies through patterns is said to be a top-down approach (from abstract legal concepts identified by experts, to their concretization in the legal documents under examination)" which was insightfully noted in an article in the journal of *Legal Knowledge and Information Systems*, "Legal Knowledge Extraction for Knowledge Graph-Based Question-Answering" by Francesco Sovrano, Monica Palmirani, and Fabio Vitali.

A missing link of sorts involves being able to connect the KG and the ODP (a challenging gap).

Efforts are underway to create a type of bridge or hinge, per these researchers: "This is why we propose to exploit the best of these two approaches by using a sort of ontological hinge that should be able to connect a bottom-up KG with top-down ODPs. In order to obtain this ontological hinge, we have to abstract new relations between the concepts of the ODPs and those of the extracted KG."

Conclusion

To make advances in AI-based legal reasoning, we'll need to use and integrate together a wide variety of legal-oriented technological components. It might seem overly buzzwordy, but we can make even just a little bit of semantics go a long way by hooking up those LKGs with those LODPs.

By gosh, that is indeed a mouthful.

.

Note: *For supplemental materials depicting the aspects discussed in this chapter, refer to Appendix B, which contains various augmented diagrams, charts, and additional related facets of relevance.*

CHAPTER 18

AI & LAW: EXTRA-LEGAL KNOWLEDGE

Key briefing points about this essay:

- Judges make use of extra-legal knowledge during their judicial decision-making
- This extra-legal knowledge can contain all sorts of problematic elements
- Trying to resort to using judicial common sense is a vague and potentially unsupported aspect
- AI-based legal reasoning systems will presumably need to encompass extra-legal knowledge
- Overall AI efforts to embody common sense are still in their infancy and wholly incomplete

Introduction

As an attorney, you undoubtedly find yourself trying to guess what is in the mind of a judge during your courtroom endeavors. You can focus on the strictly legal machinations, but that alone won't be sufficient. There are also the latitudes afforded a judge in terms of outstretched judicial decision-making beyond the purity of the law itself.

Consider the following example.

A judge opts to quickly settle a contentious motion during a trial by resorting to declaring that the matter is rather obvious as per common sense and the judge rules accordingly. The attorneys seemingly take this in stride. One of the attorneys is especially pleased and doesn't want to look any further into the mouth of this gift horse that perchance went their way. The opposing attorney, having essentially lost on this particular round, shrugs it off as simply being the way that judges sometimes rule, namely you can't win them all and you have to take your lumps from time to time.

Let's back up a moment and review that in slow motion.

Akin to revisiting a referee or umpire making a real-time play call during a football or baseball game, consider what just happened before our very eyes. I think that these legal researchers succinctly said it best: "Judges frequently experience factual 'gaps' they need to fill in order to reach a decision" (per the fascinating article entitled "Judicial Decision-Making and 'Outside' Extra-Legal Knowledge: Breaking Down Silos" by Kylie Burns, Rachel Dioso-Villac, and Zoe Rathus in the *Griffith Law Review*).

This kind of filling in that takes place by judges, doing so as part of the legal factual record of a given case, can generically be referred to as the deployment of *extra-legal knowledge*.

As further elaboration about extra-legal knowledge, consider how the mindful authors of this research concerning judicial decision-making opt to characterize the plethora of nuances involved: "Extra-legal (or exogenous) knowledge from other disciplines comes into the law in a wide array of ways: through expert evidence, through judicial 'common-sense' assumptions, as a matter of judicial notice, through parties' submissions, through the media, through interveners and amicus curiae, and through self-selection by judges themselves."

What is even perhaps more daunting or at least eyebrow-raising is this observation: "In the age of Google and Wikipedia, it has never been easier for judges to self-sourced this information." Thus, the point is that a judge might cherry-pick from a wide array of sources whatever they judicially believe is sensible and appropriate. Abundant research on this showcases that at times a judge can ruinously oversimplify complex concepts and turn the complexity into misleading simplistic mush. On top of that, a judge can imbue into those other salient inputs their own specific preferences and value-laden biases.

It is a judicial stew that can end up with all manner of oddball, misconstrued, and wholly idiosyncratic ingredients.

Of course, some judges defend this practice and assert that they are merely exercising personal judicial common sense. Reportedly, without the use of common sense, a trial would drag on endlessly as every time bit of the trial would get bogged down in the smallest of details. Arguments and counterarguments would rage continually, covering any word uttered and any courtroom action taken.

The other side to that coin is that this vaunted "judicial common sense" can be somewhat of a whim, baseless in terms of empirical evidence, rife with biases and stereotyping, and be a hidden and insidious root that ultimately leads to adjudication that is either weakly supported or produces outright injustice.

AI Comes Into The Extra-Legal Knowledge Picture

Speaking of common sense, anyone versed in the field of Artificial Intelligence (AI) can tell you that common sense is one of the hardest problems facing the advent of bona fide AI. You see, trying to program an AI system to embody common sense is an immense challenge. Nobody has yet figured out how to fully attain programmatic or algorithmic capacities that approach the range and depth of human common sense.

Why do I mention that AI is kind of stuck on trying to mimic or replicate a machine-based version of common sense and common-sense reasoning?

The answer is straightforward.

If we wish to produce AI-based legal reasoning that can ultimately be on par with human lawyers and human jurists, there seemingly is a need to include machine-based common sense. We've already earlier discussed that judges employ common sense, doing so as part of the bundle of judicial ruminations that fit within the extra-legal knowledge rubric.

AI-based legal reasoning would presumably need to encompass the same facility. I doubt that we would find any AI legal reasoning system especially worthy of use in the practice of law that didn't somehow incorporate common sense capacities. This type of potentially missing element has got to be a legally endowed showstopper.

To illustrate how hard it is to develop AI that includes common sense, the most famous of such efforts is known as Cyc (artfully named as an excerpted portion from the word "encyclopedia"). The effort to build Cyc began in 1984 and continues to this very day, making it the longest-running AI project focused on common sense computerized embodiment. Per generally revealed statistics, Cyc has over 25 million entries that seek to capture a semblance of common-sense facts and rules.

When the project began, the belief was that at least 100 million entries would be required for attaining a viable morsel of alleged common sense. After a thirty-five years long haul, the wildly guessed lower bound is still a far distance in the future. As such, some skeptics and cynics say the Cyc effort should toss in the towel and give up on a futile approach (alternative approaches are floating around and clamoring that there are better ways to solve this problem).

Conclusion

All told, we must face the reality that judges and judicial decision-making are rampant with extra-legal knowledge. Any attempt to craft AI to serve in the same capacity must also contain some of that extra-legal knowledge, though perhaps we can cut out the rubbish or biased portions.

But that desirable excising is merely icing on the cake right now since we first need to find a means to make the cake per se.

Note: *For supplemental materials depicting the aspects discussed in this chapter, refer to Appendix B, which contains various augmented diagrams, charts, and additional related facets of relevance.*

CHAPTER 19

AI & LAW: HUMAN LAWYERS AHEAD

Key briefing points about this essay:

- There is no disputing that human lawyers are well-beyond AI-based legal reasoning today
- Developers are striving mightily to get AI toward achieving on par lawyering to attorneys
- Some contend that human lawyers will never be exceeded by such AI systems
- To ponder this question, we can consider the overall notion of AI versus human intelligence
- The presumably subsumed question about lawyers is somewhat shaped accordingly

Introduction

Running a marathon has certainly become a national pastime.

The runners at the front are usually quite versed in running. One form of excitement, though also potentially a disappointment, involves a frontrunner that scoots past everyone else and largely distances themselves from the rest of the pack. They are the frontrunner that steadfastly and unyieldingly remains the frontrunner throughout the entire race.

By definition, we can likely agree that the frontrunner presumably is indeed always at the front. Of course, the frontrunner can change hats, in the sense that a runner from behind edges and goes past the existent frontrunner. What I'm trying to indicate is that it is conceivable that at some point in time a particular frontrunner might not be at the front. They could potentially lag behind and be exceeded by some other newly anointed frontrunner. Imagine that there was once a frontrunner of person A, and subsequently, the frontrunner is person B.

I trust there is no undue dispute about such a possibility.

Under what conditions might a frontrunner *always* be at the front and never relinquish the vaunted title of being the frontrunner?

In the case of AI in the law, some pundits insist the venerated human lawyer will always be the frontrunner. Any form of AI-based legal reasoning system will never catch and nor go past the likes of human attorneys. In essence, human attorneys will stridently and unerringly always be a step ahead of the advent of AI in the law.

This ostensibly appears to be a rather brazen claim.

The Conundrum About AI Versus Humans

Let's briefly explore the fervent opinion that human attorneys will continually be the frontrunner in a legally minded footrace between AI and humans.

First, consider broadening the discussion momentarily to explore the overarching question of whether human intelligence will eternally be ahead of AI. It would generally seem to logically follow that if human intelligence all told kept ahead of AI, we could reasonably infer that human lawyers would ergo be ahead of AI-based legal reasoning systems.

I realize there are counterarguments to that convenience of simplification, so we'll revisit that key assumption in a moment.

According to an analysis of AI versus human intelligence, researcher Kazimierz Trzęsicki identifies this tentative conclusion: "The result of our considerations can be put simply: human intelligence will be always a step ahead of machine intelligence" (in the journal *Studies In Logic, Grammar, And Rhetoric*, a 2016 article entitled "Can AI Be Intelligent"). Furthermore, work by the famous mathematician and expert on computability theory, Emil Post, dating from 1965 is indicated as proffering a similar stance: "All we can say is that man cannot construct a machine which can do all the thinking he can" (as mentioned in the paper "Absolute Unsolvable Problems And Relatively Undecidable Proposition" of the edited collection by Martin Davis, *The Undecidable: Basic Papers On Undecidable Propositions, Unsolvable Problems, And Computable Functions*).

There are a variety of intriguing arguments underlying this heated debate.

One argument is what I refer to as the teacher-pupil contention. The claim is made that humans are the teachers of AI. The teacher is presumed as always smarter than the pupil. Therefore, no matter how far along we advance AI, our capacity as the teacher will always keep us one foot or more ahead of the pupil. AI will never catch up.

As a counterargument, I dare say we can all think of instances whereby a pupil ultimately exceeded the apparent intellectual prowess of a teacher. It seems relatively fair to suggest that Einstein likely surpassed some of his teachers.

I realize this is all somewhat muddied by the notion of what intelligence consists of, along with how intelligence is expressed. Without getting mired in those weeds, we'll just for now take an informal viewpoint and willingly stipulate that we are being somewhat loosey-goosey on the meaning and definition of intelligence.

Another argument in favor of humans always being the frontrunner is the rather clever twist that mankind can leverage whatever AI that mankind devises. I call this the duet theory. The notion is that a human can supplement their intelligence by using an AI system. This implies that in a "1+1=2" kind of way, humans will always be greater than AI by itself.

Admittedly, that seems unbeatable. We always say that two heads are better than one. Not wanting to seem dour, but suppose that one of the heads misleads, undercuts, or otherwise disrupts the other head? In that sense, you could seemingly suggest that two heads are not even as good as one, perhaps being less than one when combined together (a human might hold back or undermine the AI). There are additional counterarguments about the viability of the duet concept.

An especially outstretched argument for humans as the never-ending frontrunner tries to invoke evolution. The declaration is made that evolution begets more intelligence and that humans will become increasingly intelligent due to evolution. I trust that we can all acknowledge the arguable elements of that proclaimed declaration. Can we really absolutely say that evolution begets more intelligence, unassailability so? What is the pace at which this evolutionary change will occur? Etc.

Even if there is a modicum of truth to the evolutionary notion, we seem to be neglecting or forgetting that AI is potentially malleable and subject to becoming increasingly able to exhibit intelligence. It seems you could make a convincing counterargument that the pace of the AI becoming more intelligent could potentially exceed the traditional evolutionary pace of human increases in intelligence (in fact, some worry that humans will become less intelligent over time due to leaning on AI to do the thinking for us, so to speak).

The bottom-line to all of this is that the question of whether human intelligence will always be the frontrunner in comparison to the decidedly second-place AI of today is a wide-open unresolved matter. For any argument favoring that supposition, there are equally valid counterarguments.

Conclusion

A final thought for now.

I promised that I would revisit the other entanglement that perhaps the legal acumen of human lawyers is not quite the same contested issue as of overall human intelligence. In essence, we could still have the prevailing condition that human intelligence exceeds AI, yet meanwhile, have AI-based legal reasoning systems that exceed the legal prowess of human attorneys.

Sorry if that seems glum, but don't worry since there are lots of arguments and counterarguments underlying that premise. For now, human lawyers reign supreme over AI-based lawyering, and you can proudly keep your head high.

Well, at least for now.

Note: *For supplemental materials depicting the aspects discussed in this chapter, refer to Appendix B, which contains various augmented diagrams, charts, and additional related facets of relevance.*

CHAPTER 20

AI & LAW:

AI-COMPLETENESS

Key briefing points about this essay:

- Today's AI is handy in solving some problems but unable to solve many more problems
- In the computer science realm, these are oft referred to as AI-hard problems
- Another phrasing is that such problems fall into the AI-completeness category
- The question of interest is whether legal reasoning is within those spheres
- There seems little doubt that full legal reasoning is AI-hard and in AI-completeness

Introduction

Be careful in believing the things you hear or see that depict today's AI as magically sentient or attaining a capability along those lines. You are being fed a heaping plate chock-full of hype.

We have to keep a level head about the technological limitations underlying contemporary AI systems.

That's not to suggest that perhaps down the road, in a somewhat distant future, we might be unable to do better and proffer AI of greater capacities. I freely admit that I am part of the AI developer milieu that is striding avidly in that direction. The thing is, nobody can say when we will have miraculous breakthroughs that will push AI closer to the bounds of human intelligence.

The insider expression of something being *AI-hard* is used to signify problems that AI is seemingly unsuitable to solve. Essentially, such problems are construed as hard or quite challenging, and getting AI to do much about them is a headscratcher. Note that these are usually within the realm of human solvable problems, such that humans using human intelligence can solve them. A different class of problems would be ones that neither human intelligence and nor AI seems to be able to solve.

Another piece of vernacular is to say that we are faced with an *AI-completeness* dilemma.

Allow me a moment to explain that outwardly enigmatic verbiage.

Those within the halls of computer science have for many years studied computer-based uses and referred to mathematical and computational models as possessing a semblance of either completeness or incompleteness. For example, mathematical logic is said to be "complete" when every theory within that stated theory is entirely provably semantically valid. This concept was generally pioneered by the famous logician Kurt Godel in the 1930s and spawned important theorems entailing both completeness and incompleteness machinations.

Nowadays, it is customary to say that there is a class of problems that we can ascribe as being within the AI-completeness conundrum. The belief is that any problem that falls within the AI-completeness category seems to presently defy being solved by existing AI.

The hope is that AI advances will gradually reduce the volume of problems that are currently in the sphere of AI completeness. Of course, another possibility is that we discover some means to simplify the inclusionary problem per se, ergo such problems no longer need the highest caliber AI to be solved.

The easiest way to think of this is that if we were to throw the proverbial AI kitchen sink at a problem and not be able to have a computer undertake satisfactorily that problem, we could assert that the problem is within the AI-completeness rubric and is summarily AI-hard. The kitchen sink could include the use of Machine Learning (ML), Knowledge-Based Systems (KBS), Natural Language Processing (NLP), and everything else in the AI grab-bag of techniques and technologies.

AI And Legal Reasoning Come Face To Face

Why am I dragging you through this murky affair about what is presumably AI-easy versus AI-hard?

Simply put, there is an open question about where the advent of full AI-based legal reasoning sits in the AI-completeness realm.

You see, we know of course that human attorneys carry out legal reasoning. This is not perfectly performed by all, nor can you say that it is perfectly done at any given point in time. But the overall sense is that human lawyers do practice law and they ostensibly do so by leveraging legal reasoning. Attorneys go to law school to learn legal reasoning, they take tests, have to showcase their legal prowess among their peers and jurists, and otherwise are called upon to dutifully and properly exercise legal reasoning.

Efforts are underway to get AI to do the same.

The popularized phrasing is that there are endeavors toward attaining a robo-lawyer (this is an unwelcome phrase by purists within the field). Please know that we are not anywhere close to achieving an AI-based legal reasoning system that would be on par with the likes of bona fide human lawyers.

On an informal basis, the fact that we don't yet have a full AI-based legal reasoning capacity that meets or exceeds human performance levels is a judicious sign that such a problem can be labeled as being within AI-completeness. Any devout legal researcher or AI builder would gladly tell you that legal reasoning via a machine is an AI-hard thing to accomplish.

There are more formalized ways of characterizing AI completeness.

A now-classic approach was devised by computer scientists Dafna Shahaf and Eyal Amir at the University of Illinois at Urbana-Champaign in 2007 when they published their paper entitled "Towards A Theory Of AI Completeness" (presented at the 8th International Symposium on Logical Formalizations of Commonsense Reasoning). They proffer this vital notion: "In this paper, we propose a new model of computation, which includes a human in the loop. This model leads to a novel classification of computational problems, based on the way the work can be split between a human and a computer – that is, how much of the computational burden is delegated to the computer; this classification is suited for a theoretical investigation of AI."

Briefly, they sketch a thought experiment involving a black box that contains both an AI system and a human (the human embodying human intelligence). Any problem fed into this black-box can be sought to be solved by either the AI or the human, for which the human steps in when the AI is at its wit's end (a bit of an anthropomorphic pun). Thus, as the researchers indicate: "Those measures examine ways in which computational workload can be split between the computer and the human oracle: our intuition is that a problem is hard if we cannot solve it without having the human perform a substantial part of the computation."

Conclusion

Step by step, the aim within the intertwining of AI and the law is to squeeze down the need for human lawyering interventions such that the AI by itself can ultimately and inevitably perform legal tasks.

We've got a lot of squeezing yet to be figured out.

Note: *For supplemental materials depicting the aspects discussed in this chapter, refer to Appendix B, which contains various augmented diagrams, charts, and additional related facets of relevance.*

CHAPTER 21

AI & LAW: FORENSIC AI TECHNO-BABBLE

Key briefing points about this essay:

- A recent prominent trial was momentarily bogged down by AI algorithms questions
- In this case, the matter related to forensic artifacts being submitted into evidence
- The particulars had to do with digital enlargement of a photo as video-excerpted
- None of the attorneys and nor the "expert" forensic witness were versed in this
- Astute lawyers should be preparing themselves for such circumstances

Introduction

A recent prominent criminal trial taking place in Wisconsin got bogged down due to questions surrounding forensic artifacts being submitted formally into evidence. As I'll momentarily explain, a key underpinning of the forensic artifacts entails the likely use of AI-based algorithms.

The trial court discussions were broadcast live and video recorded online, thus you can watch the confusion and misunderstandings directly by observing online copies of the trial (these particular matters arose on the last day before closing arguments, though continued to arise subsequently in arguments made before the judge and outside the presence of the jury).

Here's what occurred in the courtroom.

The prosecution sought to introduce some enlarged digital photos based on a video recording pertaining to the matters at hand. The prosecution hoped to use the enlarged digital photos to impeach the defendant's statements made while testifying earlier in the trial. The defense aimed to prevent the enlarged digital photos from being formally allowed into the trial.

Note that the enlarged digital photos were not previously made available by the prosecution and the defense argued that this was a form of sudden surprise as a proffering of said materials. Nonetheless, the judge opted to hear outside the presence of the jury the arguments of both sides concerning the enlarged digital photos.

As a technologist versed in legal aspects, I would say that at this point the matter went off the rails, so to speak.

Here's why.

First, the attorneys on both sides of the case had absolutely no clue about what they were arguing. They basically spewed techno-babble about the digital machinations underlying the enlarged photos. On the one hand, you cannot blame them for this difficulty since they are lawyers and seemingly not especially technology-versed. The judge was in a similar boat and freely admitted that the technical discussion that ensued was well beyond his grasp of the technological particulars.

The judge though did assert that he was versed in logic and logical arguments, which ostensibly would be sufficient to consider the matter (as you'll see in a moment, this is not necessarily the case).

Second, the prosecution brought to the witness stand an "expert" from the state that was purportedly trained in, certified in, and experienced in forensic imaging and video analysis. Upon questioning by the defense, this expert ultimately admitted that he was not as much of an expert on these matters when it came to the underlying programs per se (the judge was even surprised by this admission, and he directly asked the expert what he did at least know).

All told, the defense ended up missing an opportunity to saliently persuade the judge to not allow the enlarged digital photos to be admitted into evidence (I'll tell you how, momentarily).

The attorneys on both sides proffered rather brittle and cringe-worthy arguments, and it all eventually devolved into the judge looking at the materials with his own eyes, apparently believing that he could via his naked eye alone assess the validity of the enlarged digital photos.

Sigh.

Allow me a moment to retrace the arguments being fostered and arm you with some potentially useful technological insights that could make the difference if you ever find yourself embroiled in a similar dispute at or before trial.

The place to start is by considering that the stated technological endeavor involved grabbing a still frame from the video and then using digital tools to enlarge the frame, thus producing a large-sized picture that would purportedly showcase the existent details that could not immediately be seen via watching the video itself. The particular circumstance involved the body position of the defendant as depicted in the video, but please realize that the video was recorded at a significant distance from the defendant and was captured by a flying drone. Any ordinary visual review of the video "as is" would tend to be unable to see the defendant in any clear-cut manner.

The question then arises as to whether the enlarged digital photo is an apt and accurate representation of whatever was recorded on the video. As you might imagine, the prosecution fervently argued that it was. The defense sought to prevent the photo from being admitted, and ergo their position was that the enlarged digital photo was a distortion or contrivance or otherwise not an apt and accurate representation of the video scene.

We now can shift into high gear and consider the underlying AI algorithms that come to play in these digital image manipulations. This was something far beyond the knowledge of the attorneys, the judge, and even the state's expert on forensic image analysis.

Counting Up The Loopholes

The state's expert explained that the digital tool being used was a standard and well-accepted software package and implied thusly that it was to be fully trusted (loophole #1). Then the state's expert indicated that he had not supposedly manipulated the original frame and had only digitally enlarged it (loophole #2). When asked how the software did this digital enlargement, at first some techno-jargon was used by the state's expert, indicating that the techniques involved (get ready for some intimidating techno-lingo) nearest neighbor, bilinear, and bicubic methods (loophole #3).

The defense could have fallen into the trap of this techno-jargon and seemingly acquiesced on the matter since it sure sounded very expert-like, but they mindfully asked how those techniques actually work. The state's expert said he did not know and was unaware of how the underlying algorithms worked, nor how the software implemented those algorithms (loophole #4 and loophole #5).

For brevity herein, I'll just briefly explain the loopholes in the above logic.

Loophole #1: Merely because the software is considered to be a standard and well-accepted does not give it an always-right and purity of correctness stamp-of-approval. There could be latent errors in the software, the latest release might have newly introduced bugs or other issues, etc.

***Loophole #2*:** The expert said he did not manipulate the frame, but this is solely based on his user-oriented commands to the software. He has no idea what the software under-the-hood actually did. He assumes that his commands were unerringly and strictly obeyed. Nonsense.

Loophole #3: The cited generic algorithmic methods vary dramatically as to which variant algorithm is specifically implemented, plus there is a vast difference between the theory of what an algorithm contains versus how it was computer programmed into the software being used. Be wary of this.

***Loophole #4 and #5*:** The state's expert admitted upon questioning that he didn't know the underlying program code. This was a veritable Mac truck that the defense missed an erstwhile opportunity to drive wide through. In short, this admission meant that by-and-large everything else the expert said about the enlargement was tainted and doubtful as to how it was done and what it produced.

I could barely contain myself as this unfolded in real-time while I was watching the case online. In a polite way of phrasing, this was akin to the blind leading the blind (inclusive of the attorneys, the judge, the expert).

There were plenty of other guffaws and exasperatingly nonsensical aspects that arose on this.

For example, the state's expert and the prosecution repeatedly insisted that the work had been double-checked as part of the standard operating procedures, which was said to have been done by another presumably similar "expert" of the state.

This is loophole #6.

***Loophole #6*.** If the expert already in the court was unaware of how the algorithm functions and nor how the underlying code works, we might naturally assume that the double-checking was done by an akin expert (you'd ask about this). You see, you could line up a thousand of these "experts" and have them all attest to the enlargement, but that apparent reinforcing volume is wholly misleading since they are all equally unaware (this is akin to adding zero plus zero, namely it is still irrefutably zero).

Conclusion

All told, I kept watching and eventually counted up to loophole #10 and finally gave up trying to mull over this snippet of the case. It was rather painful to watch.

Hopefully, this instance will spur you to make sure to have in your back pocket the needed technological legally oriented arguments and counterarguments for the day that you find yourself in any similar situation about AI algorithms, whichever side of the case you perchance are on.

Note: *For supplemental materials depicting the aspects discussed in this chapter, refer to Appendix B, which contains various augmented diagrams, charts, and additional related facets of relevance.*

CHAPTER 22

AI & LAW:

NO VEHICLES IN THE PARK

Key briefing points about this article:

- A simple catchphrase with a lot of legal debate history is this: *No vehicles in the park*
- This acrimonious debate got launched in 1958 and has stood the test of time
- Key to this is the qualms over "vehicle" and the meaning of the words and phrase
- This is a strawman for considering the myriad of ways that we can interpret language
- AI-based legal reasoning is faced with the same conundrum (there's no escaping it)

Introduction

Envision a seemingly familiar phrase that turns out to have a ton of hidden meaning and has been repeatedly probed, stretched, and perhaps overly examined as though akin to the proverbial beating of a dead horse.

This notable and at times rancorous phrase is only five words in length.

Here it is: *No vehicles in the park.*

Your reaction is either one of ho-hum as though this is old hat or one of excited response to a catchphrase that has entered into legal lore as having a demonstrative role in the history of the law and lofty debates about the nature of law.

Yes, for those of you that are utterly steeped in the law and that consider yourselves as somewhat of a legal scholar or devoted legal beagle of outstretched legal debates, you most certainly recognize those five words. In fact, you might be ready to go to fisticuffs with other lawyers regarding the devout meaning of that phrase. Those of you that perchance fully know the entire history and claimed import of the phrase are undoubtedly weary of it and wish that the whole hullabaloo was a bit less overblown.

I realize that some of you might be scratching your head and wondering why the phrase is ostensibly such a big deal. You would naturally and sensibly assume that this kind of plain wording has appeared in many laws and that it is altogether rather straightforward. Simply stated, it would seem that a particular park that otherwise is open and available to people has a restriction that clearly states there shall be no vehicles permitted within that park.

Case closed.

Not so easy on that case closed, I'm sorry to report.

Let's unpack the matter.

Back in 1958, the *Harvard Law Review* opted to publish a debate between two highly regarded law school professors, namely Oxford's H.L.A. Hart and Harvard's Lon Fuller. Hart provided a hypothetical possibility of a newly enacted law regarding a public park. The made-up law would succinctly state that there shall be no vehicles in the park.

At first glance, it seems abundantly plausible that such a law might be enacted. I think we can all reasonably agree that there isn't anything bizarre or outlandish about such a law being placed onto the books.

As with most things in life, and especially in the legal profession, the devil is in the details.

For example, what does the word "vehicle" mean?

The assumption might seem to be readily apparent, specifically that automobiles are not allowed in the park. The underlying logical basis for this assumption is that people are presumed to need safety in their use of the park, such as walking to and fro, and ergo it would be prudent to prevent automobiles from entering into the park. Disallowing automobiles would aid in reducing the chances of an injurious or deadly collision between a person in the park and a car that opted to be driven in the park.

Fuller retorted to Hart's example by pointing out that the word "vehicle" is quite ambiguous and therefore there is a lot of legal murkiness to be dealt with: "Having in mind what was sought by the regulation concerning parks, ought it to be considered as barring tricycles? When questions of this sort are decided there is at least an 'intersection' of 'is' and since the judge, in deciding what the rule 'is,' does 'ought,' so in the light of his notions of what 'it ought to be' in order to carry out its purpose" (*Harvard Law Review*, February 1958, "Positivism and Fidelity to Law: A Reply to Professor Hart").

In short, the question arises as to whether "vehicle" refers solely to automobiles, or might it also include tricycles, bicycles, wheeled carts, and even petite toy cars that a child might play with. A Pandora's box is contained within and ultimately torn wide open due to the jampacked notion of what a vehicle might mean.

Does this law truly encompass tricycles, toy cars, and other marginally threatening types of vehicles?

Furthermore, Fuller asks whether a World War II truck that is to be mounted on a pedestal in the park as a memorial would be considered prohibited by the no-vehicles rule.

Legal Semantic Indeterminism And AI In The Law

The broader point is that the words used in our laws are oftentimes vague and require preferably definitive and more ironclad boundaries. The "no vehicles in the park" catchphrase have become a convenient strawman in zillions of legal debates about how we should interpret our laws. As legal researcher Frederick Schauer indicated in his extensive review of this ongoing debate: "It is the most famous hypothetical in the common law world. And it is part of one of the more memorable debates in the history of jurisprudence. Stunning in its simplicity, H.L.A. Hart's example of a rule prohibiting vehicles from a public park was intended primarily as a response to the claims of the legal realists about the indeterminacy of legal rules" (*NYU Law Review* article entitled "A Critical Guide To Vehicles In The Park).

For skeptics or cynics that proclaim no such legally ambiguous case would ever occur, they are often directed to look at the U.S. Supreme Court case of *Lozman v. City of Riviera Beach, Florida* (2013), which involved whether Lozman's floating home was legally considered a vessel and thus bound by federal maritime jurisdictions (SCOTUS ruled 7-2 that Lozman's floating home was not a "vessel" for purposes of 1 U.S.C 3).

What a crazy world we live in that a handful of words or even just one word is so loosey-goosey.

Into this sordid or some say healthy debate about words comes AI.

If we are going to use AI in the law, what expectations should we have about how AI systems are to deal with ambiguous language exemplified by the park circumstance? Humans already struggle with the meaning, including attorneys, and we need to clarify what an AI legal reasoning system is supposed to do too.

Our use of natural languages such as English is replete with pervasive vagueness and open texture. Suppose a modern-day drone is autonomously flown over the park, does that constitute a "vehicle" and is it within the confines of being "in the park" as per the stated law?

Conclusion

An AI system has no magic wand to overcome the semantic indeterminate facets of human language. One of the tough hurdles for devising AI-based legal reasoning entails finding algorithmic ways to consider and cope with such semantic indeterminism.

Meanwhile, please keep your vehicles out of the park.

Note: *For supplemental materials depicting the aspects discussed in this chapter, refer to Appendix B, which contains various augmented diagrams, charts, and additional related facets of relevance.*

CHAPTER 23

AI & LAW: AI ROBO-JURORS

Key briefing points about this essay:

- There is widespread discussion about attaining AI-based lawyering
- In addition, there is some discussion about achieving AI-based jurists
- It is nearly taboo to whisper about the future possibility of AI-based so-called robo-jurors
- We trace the history of juries and the ongoing conundrum about jury composition
- If AI rose to the suitable level of serving as a juror, would this even be allowed?

Introduction

There is little doubt that juries are a mainstay of our existing judicial system.

Though this might appear to be a sacrosanct and unwavering legal construct, we can set aside for the moment the rock bed of juries all told and consider some creative out-of-the-box thinking.

When it comes to adjudication and the use of a jury, there are two fundamental questions to be addressed:

1) Should or should we not even have juries at all?
2) If we opt to have juries then the next aspect asks what is the suitable composition of a jury?

These might seem on the surface as readily answerable, especially the first question.

The use of juries traces historically to at least the eighth century and has generally remained relatively variously accepted since then. British common law decidedly contained provisions for the use of juries and those principally carried overall into American law. The U.S. Constitution and the U.S. Supreme Court have plenty of clear-cut declarations about the core guarantee of the right to a jury trial in most criminal cases, though of course, the matter of a jury for civil cases is quite less demonstrative.

You could try to argue that the mandated use of a jury is somewhat rocky because there is not one blanket requirement that juries always must be used in all matters of jurisprudence. Yes, there is a bit of a loophole on that definitiveness, but let's agree that there is still an iota or greater of a proclaimed existence for the use of juries. Thus, it seems we can safely announce that we should use juries, albeit when certain kinds of circumstances warrant them.

Shifting attention to the second question, there has been quite a lot of angst and hand wringing over the desirable composition for juries and the selection of jurors thereof. During the twelfth century, jurors also served as witnesses during trials and could also ask questions of other witnesses. In the fourteenth century, the nature of jurors gradually transformed into becoming solely triers of fact.

You can ostensibly claim that we take a somewhat curious view of what a juror is supposed to be and do: "The traditional view of the juror's role throughout trial is that of an empty vessel into which information presented in the form of exhibits, testimony, argument, and judicial instructions will be poured" (as stated in the book *The Jury Process* by Nancy Marder, 2005).

Humans though aren't empty vessels, they are instead filled with all kinds of knowledge, opinions, and human behavioral foibles. On top of that murkiness, you can include that jurors are by and large clueless when it comes to being a trier of fact.

The crux here is that we prefer that our jurors do not have any special capability as a juror and otherwise purposely seek out those that essentially are oblivious as to the triers of facts role. Per legal researcher William Schwarz: "The jury trial, at best, is the apotheosis of the amateur. Why should anyone think that twelve persons brought in from the street, selected in various ways, for their lack of general ability, should have any special capacity for deciding controversies between persons" (in the Foreword to the book *The Jury: Tools of Kings* by Lloyd Moore, 1973).

You might already be aware that for quite a while there was a preference to avert having jurors that came from a professional background. For example, a juror that was a medical doctor might overstep during jury deliberations and sway the other jurors about medical-related evidence presented at trial. This use of a juror's personal expertise was seen as quite worrisome since it occurs outside the presence of the court and becomes generally an unknown or somewhat unchallengeable element for the attorneys.

According to studies of so-called "professional jurors" (ones that come from a profession), a dominant viewpoint today is that they seem to enrich the jury composition: "Indeed, ideally a jury *pools* the community's experiences and wisdom in order to determine critical issues at trial -- this is one of the anchoring visions of late twentieth-century jury reform. The jury system has power largely because jurors do bring unique and differing sets of life experiences to the table. By definition, these life experiences contain some sort of specialized knowledge in the sense that other jurors who have not had these experiences do not share that knowledge" (in *Yale Law & Policy Review*, Michael Mushlin, "Bound And Gagged: The Peculiar Predicament Of Professional Jurors").

Ongoing debates ensue about employing jurors as a particular job function whereby we can say that they would be "expert jurors" that are especially versed in the trier of fact role.

Categories Of Jurors And Expansion Thereof

Let's go ahead and focus on jurors as composed into a jury, and categorize them in this manner:

1) Lay jurors only (non-professional plus professional)
2) Expert jurors only (explicitly versed and employed as jurors)
3) Hybrid juries (a mix of lay jurors plus expert jurors)

As a twist that maybe catches you by surprise, some have proposed that we will inevitably be able to count AI as a potential juror too. These are colloquially referred to as robo-jurors.

Using AI in the capacity of a juror is seemingly ridiculous, some exclaim. A jury of our peers is a straightforward inviolate rule, ergo it stands to reason that juries must consist exclusively of humans. No AI allowed.

Others argue that we might use AI to overcome the human failings of human jurors. We could replace human jurors with AI-based juror systems, or we could at least augment human jurors with such AI.

Envision that we could end up with these possibilities for jury compositions:

1) AI and Lay human jurors (using AI-based juror systems)
2) AI and Expert human jurors (using AI-based juror systems)
3) AI and Hybrid juries (using AI-based juror systems)
4) AI-only jurors (entirely and solely AI-based juror systems)

You would be hard-pressed to find anything in the Federalist's papers supporting this added aspect of tossing AI into the jury pool. Of course, the counterargument is that the advent of AI was not foreseeable at that prior time and we need to keep up with the new advances made feasible via high-tech.

Conclusion

Could we someday have AI serving in the highly venerated capacity of a juror?

Judging by today's AI facilities, this seems doubtful, though if we were somehow able to craft AI for this role, whether we would constitutionally allow it is a whole other can of worms.

Note: *For supplemental materials depicting the aspects discussed in this chapter, refer to Appendix B, which contains various augmented diagrams, charts, and additional related facets of relevance.*

CHAPTER 24

AI & LAW:
TRIFECTA OF AI LAW ROLES

Key briefing points about this essay:

- You might be willing to accept the notion of someday having AI-based robo-lawyers
- It might also cross your mind that we could end up with AI-based robo-judges
- Stretching this legal landscape to include AI-based robo-jurors might seem churlish
- Anyway, you could say the three constructs might form a type of legal AI trifecta
- Perhaps wildly optimistic, we can nonetheless give the matter some thought

Introduction

I'm betting that you've used the word *trifecta* from time to time.

We use this handy word for just about anything that seems as going against quite staggering odds. This all began when *trifecta* was coined to depict horse racing bets that managed to miraculously choose the first place, second place, and third place winners, doing so in each respective winning position and altogether in their correct order.

It is a hard bet to win.

Of course, you can be somewhat argumentative and make the case that sometimes the top three are rather clear-cut choices. On top of that, perhaps it is already well-known as to the capabilities of those top three. By and large, you could say that the odds of calling a trifecta might be more manageable if there is a lot of preconditions that are somehow divined.

Nonetheless, there is always the opportunity for the vagaries of chance to spoil things, assuming that an overt fix isn't already in the cards. Surely, the trifecta is not especially impressive if each of the jockeys is paid off or otherwise induced to ensure that the three designated horses arrive in the one-two-three finishing order.

We take it as a base assumption that a trifecta is amazingly triumphant since the bet was made in a milieu of random chance. Out of the zillions of permutations, a trifecta betting winner got wildly lucky and can try to claim it was skill alone, though we are apt to believe that their ship happened to land successfully on that day and in that instance.

Shifting gears, let's consider another kind of trifecta, one that some believe could eventually occur in the practice of law.

I'm obliquely referring to the advent of AI-based legal reasoning. There are ongoing efforts to construct AI systems that can undertake the tasks of lawyering. So far, this has proven to be a quite challenging problem. Any human lawyer can pat themselves on the back for how hard it is to mimic or simulate the practice of law via the use of a computer alone. Getting AI to do the legal wrangling of attorneys is an extremely difficult endeavor and we do not ostensibly know when or if there will be devised AI that can be anywhere on par with human lawyers.

Betting For Or Against A Legal AI Trifecta

Despite that perhaps gloomy outlook about whether AI will inevitably attain lawyering acumen, we can still remain buoyant and hotly continue the pursuit. Imagine that there are sufficient breakthroughs in AI technologies that slip us closer to the legal beagle prowess range. We can put on our thinking caps and try to assess what that future might consist of.

The most discussed and likeliest first winner in the horse race toward infusing AI into the law would be the likes of AI-based robo-lawyers. As a side warning, those within the field of crafting such AI are somewhat leery of and find loathsome the catchphrase of robo-lawyer. I use it here with caution and acknowledgment that it is a potential misnomer (the same goes for any of the robo-related nicknames).

What else is there besides the vaunted AI-based robo-lawyer?

Coming in at second place is the rise of the AI-based robo-judge.

Yes, the idea is that we would have judges that aren't only humanoids. These AI-invoked judges might be relegated to only lower court levels or perhaps used in extraordinarily minor legal matters. In any case, wherever they fit in, there is at least an erstwhile quest to create them.

The third-place position might be quite surprising to you. I say this because there is little talk about this tail-end position. You see, bringing up the final member of the trifecta is the AI-based robo-juror.

A bit of a brouhaha surrounds the AI-based robo-juror notion. It is one thing to have a robo-lawyer representing a human client that perchance is AI-based. We can stretch our minds to also somewhat tolerate the use of AI as a robo-judge. But taking that cliff-hanging step into the legal abyss and anointing AI to serve as jurors is beyond the pale for many.

We hold dear the heartwarming and justice-wielding concept of a jury of *our peers*. Humans sitting as jurors in trials involving humans that are facing adjudication, that's got to be the way things are properly ordained to be. It would seem nonsensical to have AI as a juror, whereby a human defendant is dependent upon a trier of facts "peer" that is not even a human.

Anyway, we'll have to wait and see how that pans out. Perhaps we will be willing to accept some form of AI augmentation for human jurors. Or we might be open to considering a suitable AI system as being an *intellectual peer*, despite lacking the other attributes of being human (that's one of those potential legal loopholes that could be leveraged). Those arcane legal arguments though are not yet within realistic view.

The AI-based legal reasoning trifecta then comes out this way:

1) AI-based robo-lawyers
2) AI-based robo-judges
3) AI-based robo-jurors

You are certainly welcome to debate the sequence or order of the claimed winners. For example, perhaps we are able to arrive at AI-based robo-judges sooner than we can attain AI-based robo-lawyers. In that case, the top two contenders in the aforementioned sequence would need to swap positions.

Another consideration is the desire to summarily reject utterly the AI-based robo-juror construct. Take it out of the list, you might exhort. Indeed, skeptics and critics find the idea so ridiculous and impossible that it should not be ranked as a contender in this legal horse race. That means that the trifecta is busted since we are presumably down to just two horses (robo-lawyers and robo-judges).

Conclusion

Though there is a bit of whimsy about this trifecta deliberation, you can find some salient hidden points that are worthy of mindful mulling.

Would the AI used for one of the three be simply repurposed into the other two?

Or would the AI be entirely separate and distinct, such that there is no overlap involved?

And so on.

A final thought is that whatever you might argue is the sequence for the trifecta, including those that reject the trifecta as ever feasible at all, anyone putting down some dough as a bet on this is facing some mighty tall odds.

Note: *For supplemental materials depicting the aspects discussed in this chapter, refer to Appendix B, which contains various augmented diagrams, charts, and additional related facets of relevance.*

CHAPTER 25

AI & LAW: JUDGING AI JUDGES

Key briefing points about this essay:

- AI judges potentially will inevitably arise at your local neighborhood courthouse
- They might not be the robo-judges of sci-fi, but will nonetheless provide judging
- To corral what might be an AI overreach there is the idea that human judges will prevail
- All AI legal judgments will need to be reviewed and approved (or not) by a human judge
- This seems sensible but regrettably has some issues to be dealt with

Introduction

Society seems to have a great deal of fascination with the possibility of having robo-judges. This would seemingly consist of AI systems that are empowered to serve in a judicial capacity as a judge.

On the surface, the idea of having AI systems in this quite regal and vital role seems absurd. How dare we use machines to oversee and assess humans that are seeking redress in our courts? Only human judges ought to sit in the crucial position of making judgments about other humans.

Well, the retort goes, you have to admit that human judges have a lot of inherent biases and human behavioral drawbacks. We might be better off using some dispassionate AI system that will be more matter of fact, for which the AI would purely and logically leverage the law and render judgments utterly free of human whim.

Seems convincing.

Hold your horses, the counterargument replies, we already know that AI systems can contain various biases, including racial biases, gender biases, and the like. Furthermore, the arcane mathematics underlying some of the AI systems is murky and does not lend itself to proffering a logical basis for why a judgment has been generated in the fashion that it has. We could frighteningly and woefully become subject to AI computational pattern matching that is grossly unfair and fully inexplicable.

I suppose it is obvious that the back-and-forth arguments about using AI as judges are replete with debate and acrimonious accusations.

Tossing more flammable fuel into the brewing fire, an ostensibly favorable consideration is that an AI system doing judging could presumably and vastly expand access to justice.

The AI would be available online, thus reachable anywhere that someone can log in and use the judicial capacities. The odds are that the AI judge would be accessed 24x7 and potentially be much less expensive to use than human judges.

You see, some lament that today we are faced with limitations on the number and availability of human judges. Via AI, those constraints would be lifted tremendously since the automation can be replicated at the push of a button.

Whereas access to justice is currently behind the eight ball and jammed up due to the need for human labor (i.e., human judges), the leveraging of an always-on always-available and pennies on a dollar economical AI set of judges would be a boon to those seeking justice.

Crazy talk, comes the rejoinder. All that you are doing is spreading bad justice to a wider swath of the population. Under the guise of seeking to bolster justice, you will fully undercut justice while these AI systems produce inane judgments and make unsettling and unlawful proclamations.

That's quite a talking point. Alright, here's what we'll do, as a means of placating those that feel this AI judging is an overreach, we'll make sure that there is a means of checking the power of those AI judges. That ought to settle the matter.

Human judges will serve above the AI judges and put the brakes on AI judging that goes awry.

Case closed.

Exploring The AI And Human Judges Judging

Before we decide that the case is locked shut and there is nothing left to discuss, it might be helpful to keep digging deeper into this presumed solution.

Let's do so with our eyes wide open.

Adding to this concept of humans judges above AI judges, the legal research by Frank Fagan and Saul Levmore state the matter this way: "In freestyle tournaments, as well as in medical care and other settings, the human takes charge of the combinatory effort and can ignore or overrule the machine. The machine can try to overrule the human, but ultimately the next move in the freestyle game, the practice of medicine, and the operation of a conventional or autonomous car or airplane, is in the hands of the human" (as published in the Southern California Law Review in a piece entitled "The Impact Of Artificial Intelligence On Rules, Standards, and Judicial Discretion").

And to further clarify, the researchers tend to see this as more than the AI blindly or obliquely tossing legal rulings over the cubicle walls to these overseeing human judges. There will be a kind of symbiotic relationship: "Over time, combinations of humans and machines will learn how to coordinate and how often to overrule one another; a human might simply change the goal midstream in order to alter the machine's conclusion."

A valid criticism of this human judge that sits above (or astride) the AI-generated judgments will regrettably cause a further deterioration of the already limited availability of human judges. You are simply moving the chairs around on the deck of the Titanic, the outcry bellows. When you stubbornly put in place AI that is going to require human judges, you inexorably pump up and exponentially increase the demand for human judges.

Cut out the middleman, as it were, and get rid of the AI, such critics say. Focus on the true matter at hand, the need for more human judges.

Another qualm about these matters is that the human judges might fall into a mental trap of assuming that the AI must be right.

The human judges could become mindless approvers. Researchers Fagan and Levmore aim toward believing that human judges will be their own thinkers and provide the right stuff: "It makes little difference whether a modern judge uses insights offered by a modern machine, a standard constructed by an earlier lawmaker, or indeed an earlier precedent that can now be overruled. In all these cases, the combination might or might not reveal the 'reasons' for its suggestion, and the current judge is empowered to use his or her thinking to decide how much to rely on the available machine."

Conclusion

The use of AI judges seems nearly unstoppable, some contend, and so you might as well stop trying to stop it from happening. Your better option is to find a means to blend the use of AI judges and human judges, optimizing the limited human labor of human judges and maximizing the benefits of having AI-based legal reasoning systems that proffer judging facilities.

This case is decidedly not yet closed and a lot more rumination is required.

Note: *For supplemental materials depicting the aspects discussed in this chapter, refer to Appendix B, which contains various augmented diagrams, charts, and additional related facets of relevance.*

APPENDIX A
TEACHING WITH THIS MATERIAL AND BIBLIOGRAPHY

The essays in this book can readily be used as a reading supplemental to augment traditional textbook-oriented content, particularly used in a class on AI or a class about the law.

Courses where this material is most likely applicable encompass classes at a college or university level.

Here are some typical settings that might apply:

- Computer Science. Classes studying AI, or possibly a CS social impacts class, etc.

- Law. Law classes exploring technology and its adoption for legal uses.

- Sociology. Sociology classes on the adoption and advancement of technology.

Specialized classes at the undergraduate and graduate level can also make use of this material.

For each chapter, consider whether you think the chapter provides material relevant to your course topic.

There are plenty of opportunities to get the students thinking about the topics and encourage them to decide whether they agree or disagree with the points offered and positions taken.

I would also encourage you to have the students do additional research beyond the chapter material presented (I provide next some suggested assignments that they can do).

RESEARCH ASSIGNMENTS ON THESE TOPICS

Your students can find research and background material on these topics, doing so in various tech journals, law journals, and other related publications.

Here are some suggestions for homework or projects that you could assign to students:

a) Assignment for foundational AI research topics: Research and prepare a paper and a presentation on a specific aspect of AI, such as Machine Learning, ANN, etc. The paper should cite at least 3 reputable sources. Compare and contrast to what has been stated in the chosen chapter.

b) Assignment for Law topics: Research and prepare a paper covering Law aspects via at least 3 reputable sources and analyze the characterizations. Compare and contrast to what has been stated in the chosen chapter.

c) Assignment for a Business topic: Research and prepare a paper and a presentation on businesses and advanced technology regarding AI and Law. What is trending, and why? Make sure to cite at least 3 reputable sources. Compare and contrast to the depictions herein.

d) Assignment to do a Startup: Have the students prepare a paper or business plan about how they might start up a business in this realm. They could also be asked to present their business plan and should also have a prepared presentation deck to coincide with it.

You can certainly adjust the aforementioned assignments to fit your particular needs and class structure.

You'll notice that I usually suggest that (at least) 3 reputable cited sources be utilized for the paper writing-based assignments.

I usually steer students toward "reputable" publications, since otherwise, they will cite some less reliable sources that have little or no credentials, other than that they happened to appear online was easy to retrieve. You can, of course, define "reputable" in whatever way you prefer, for example, some faculty think Wikipedia is not reputable while others believe it is reputable and allow students to cite it.

The reason that I usually ask for at least 3 citations is that if the student only relies upon one or two citations, they usually settle on whatever they happened to find the fastest. By requiring 3 (or more) citations, it usually seems to inspire them to explore more extensively and likely end-up finding five or more sources, and then whittling it down to 3 if so needed.

I have not specified the length of their papers and leave that to you to tell the students what you prefer.

For each of those assignments, you could end up with a short one to two-pager or you could do a dissertation length in-depth paper. Base the length on whatever best fits for your class, and likewise the credit amount of the assignment within the context of the other grading metrics you'll be using for the class.

I usually try to get students to present their work, in addition to doing the writing. This is a helpful practice for what they will do in the business world. Most of the time, they will be required to prepare an analysis and present it. If you don't have the class time or inclination to have the students present their papers, then you can presumably omit the aspect of them putting together presentations.

GUIDE TO USING THE CHAPTERS

For each of the chapters, I provide the next some various ways to use the chapter contents.

You can assign the below tasks as individual homework assignments, or the tasks can be used for team projects. You can easily layout a series of assignments, such as indicating that the students are to do item "a" below for say Chapter 1, then "b" for the next chapter of the book, and so on.

a) What is the main point of the chapter and describe in your own words the significance of the topic.

b) Identify at least two aspects in the chapter that you agree with and support your concurrence by providing at least one other outside researched item as support; make sure to explain your basis for agreeing with the aspects.

c) Identify at least two aspects in the chapter that you disagree with and support your disagreement by providing at least one other outside researched item as support; make sure to explain your basis for disagreeing with the aspects.

d) Find an aspect that was not covered extensively in the chapter, doing so by conducting outside research, and then offer an expanded indication about how that aspect ties into the chapter, along with the added significance it brings to the topic.

e) Interview a specialist in the industry about the topic of the chapter, collect from them their thoughts and opinions, and readdress the chapter by citing your source and how they compared and contrasted to the material,

f) Interview a relevant professor or researcher in a college or university setting about the topic of the chapter, collect from them their thoughts and opinions, and readdress the chapter by citing your source and how they compared and contrasted to the material,

g) Try to update a chapter by finding out the latest on the topic and ascertain whether the issue or topic has now been solved or whether it is still being addressed, explain what you come up with.

The above are all ways in which you can get the students of your class involved in considering the material of a given chapter. You could mix things up by having one of those above assignments per each week, covering the chapters over the course of the semester or quarter.

SUGGESTED REFERENCES TO EXPLORE

To help get your students started in finding relevant and important papers on the topic of AI and the law, I provide next a handy bibliography that can be utilized.

You could also assign the students to each (or in teams) read an assigned reference from the list, and then have them provide either a written summary and review or do so as part of a classroom presentation.

BIBLIOGRAPHIC REFERENCES

1. Aleven, Vincent (1997). "Teaching Case-Based Argumentation Through a Model and Examples," Ph.D. Dissertation, University of Pittsburgh.

2. Aleven, Vincent (2003). "Using Background Knowledge in Case-Based Legal Reasoning: A Computational Model and an Intelligent Learning Environment," Artificial Intelligence.

3. Amgoud, Leila (2012). "Five Weaknesses of ASPIC+," Volume 299, Communications in Computer and Information Science (CCIS).

4. Antonious, Grigoris, and George Baryannis, Sotiris Batsakis, Guido Governatori, Livio Robaldo, Givoanni Siragusa, Ilias Tachmazidis (2018). "Legal Reasoning and Big Data: Opportunities and Challenges," August 2018, MIREL Workshop on Mining and Reasoning Legal Texts.

5. Ashley, Kevin (1991). "Reasoning with Cases and Hypotheticals in HYPO," Volume 34, International Journal of Man-Machine Studies.

6. Ashley, Kevin, and Karl Branting, Howard Margolis, and Cass Sunstein (2001). "Legal Reasoning and Artificial Intelligence: How Computers 'Think' Like Lawyers," Symposium: Legal Reasoning and Artificial Intelligence, University of Chicago Law School Roundtable.

7. Baker, Jamie (2018). "A Legal Research Odyssey: Artificial Intelligence as Disrupter," Law Library Journal.

8. Batsakis, Sotiris, and George Baryannis, Guido Governatori, Illias Tachmazidis, Grigoris Antoniou (2018). "Legal Representation and Reasoning in Practice: A Critical Comparison," Volume 313, Legal Knowledge and Information Systems.

9. Bench-Capon, Trevor (2004). "AGATHA: Automation of the Construction of Theories in Case Law Domains," January 2004, Legal Knowledge and Information Systems Jurix 2004, Amsterdam.

10. Bench-Capon, Trevor (2012). "Representing Popov v Hayashi with Dimensions and Factors," March 2012, Artificial Intelligence and Law.

11. Bench-Capon, Trevor, and Givoanni Sartor (2003). "A Model of Legal Reasoning with Cases Incorporating Theories and Values," November 2013, Artificial Intelligence.

12. Breuker, Joost (1996). "A Functional Ontology of Law," October 1996, ResearchGate.

13. Bruninghaus, Stefanie, and Kevin Ashley (2003). "Combining Case-Based and Model-Based Reasoning for Predicting the Outcome of Legal Cases," June 2003, ICCBR'03: Proceedings of the 5th International Conference on Case-based reasoning: Research and Development.

14. Buchanan, Bruce, and Thomas Headrick (1970). "Some Speculation about Artificial Intelligence and Legal Reasoning," Volume 23, Stanford Law Review.

15. Chagal-Feferkorn, Karni (2019). "Am I An Algorithm or a Product: When Products Liability Should Apply to Algorithmic Decision-Makers," Stanford Law & Policy Review.

16. Douglas, William (1948). "The Dissent: A Safeguard of Democracy," Volume 32, Journal of the American Judicature Society.

17. Dung, P, and R. Kowalski, F. Toni (2006). "Dialectic Proof Procedures for Assumption-Based Admissible Argumentation," Artificial Intelligence.

18. Eliot, Lance (2020). AI And Legal Reasoning Essentials. LBE Press Publishing.

19. Eliot, Lance (2020). Artificial Intelligence and LegalTech Essentials. LBE Press Publishing.

20. Eliot, Lance (2020). "FutureLaw 2020 Showcases How Tech is Transforming The Law, Including the Impacts of AI," April 16, 2020, Forbes.

21. Erdem, Esra, and Michael Gelfond, Nicola Leone (2016). "Applications of Answer Set Programming," AI Magazine.

22. Gardner, Anne (1987). Artificial Intelligence and Legal Reasoning. MIT Press.

23. Genesereth, Michael (2009). "Computational Law: The Cop in the Backseat," Stanford Center for Legal Informatics, Stanford University.

24. Ghosh, Mirna (2019). "Automation of Legal Reasoning and Decision Based on Ontologies," Normandie Universite.

25. Grabmair, Matthias (2017). "Predicting Trade Secret Case Outcomes using Argument Schemes and Learned Quantitative Value Effect Tradeoffs," IJCAI June 12, 2017, London, United Kingdom.

26. Hage, Jaap (1996). "A Theory of Legal Reasoning and a Logic to Match," Volume 4, Artificial Intelligence and Law.

27. Hage, Jaap (2000). "Dialectical Models in Artificial Intelligence and Law," Artificial Intelligence and Law.

28. Hage, Japp, and Ronald Leenes, Arno Lodder (1993). "Hard Cases: A Procedural Approach," Artificial Intelligence and Law.

29. Hobbes, Thomas (1651). The Matter, Form, and Power of a Common-Wealth Ecclesiasticall and Civil.

30. Holmes, Oliver (1897). "The Path of the Law," Volume 10, Harvard Law Review.

31. Katz, Daniel, and Michael Bommarito, Josh Blackman (2017). "A General Approach for Predicting the Behavior of the Supreme Court of the United States," April 12, 2017, PLOS ONE.

32. Kowalski, Robert, and Francesca Toni (1996). "Abstract Argumentation," AI-Law96.

33. Laswell, Harold (1955). "Current Studies of the Decision Process: Automation Creativity," Volume 8, Western Political Quarterly.

34. Libal, Tomer, and Alexander Steen (2019). "The NAI Suite: Drafting and Reasoning over Legal Texts," October 15, 2019, arXiv.

35. Lipton, Zachary (2017). "The Mythos of Model Interpretability," March 6, 2017, arXiv.

36. Martin, Andrew, and Kevin Quinn, Theodore Ruger, Pauline Kim (2004). "Competing Approaches to Predicting Supreme Court Decision Making," December 2014, Symposium on Forecasting U.S. Supreme Court Decisions.

37. McCarty, Thorne (1977). "Reflections on TAXMAN: An Experiment in Artificial Intelligence and Legal Reasoning," January 1977, Harvard Law Review.

38. Modgil, Sanjay, and Henry Prakken (2013). "The ASPIC+ Framework for Structured Argumentation: A Tutorial," December 16, 2013, Argument & Computation.

39. Mowbray, Andrew, and Philip Chung, Graham Greenleaf (2019). "Utilising AI in the Legal Assistance Sector," LegalAIIA Workshop, ICAIL, June 17, 2019, Montreal, Canada.

40. Parasuraman, Raja, and Thomas Sheridan, Christopher Wickens (2000). "A Model for Types and Levels of Human Interaction with Automation," May 2000, IEEE Transactions on Systems, Man, and Cybernetics.

41. Popple, James (1993). "SHYSTER: A Pragmatic Legal Expert System," Ph.D. Dissertation, Australian National University.

42. Prakken, Henry, and Giovanni Sartor (2015). "Law and Logic: A Review from an Argumentation Perspective," Volume 227, Artificial Intelligence.

43. Rissland, Edwina (1988). Artificial Intelligence and Legal Reasoning: A Discussion of the Field and Gardner's Book," Volume 9, AI Magazine.

44. Rissland, Edwina (1990). "Artificial Intelligence and Law: Stepping Stones to a Model of Legal Reasoning," Yale Law Journal.

45. Searle, John (1980). "Minds, Brains, and Programs," Volume 3, Behavioral and Brain Sciences.

46. Sunstein, Cass (2001). "Of Artificial Intelligence and Legal Reasoning," University of Chicago Law School, Public Law and Legal Theory Working Papers.

47. Sunstein, Cass, and Kevin Ashley, Karl Branting, Howard Margolis (2001). "Legal Reasoning and Artificial Intelligence: How Computers 'Think' Like Lawyers," Symposium: Legal Reasoning and Artificial Intelligence, University of Chicago Law School Roundtable.

48. Surden, Harry (2014). "Machine Learning and Law," Washington Law Review.

49. Surden, Harry (2019). "Artificial Intelligence and Law: An Overview," Summer 2019, Georgia State University Law Review.

50. Valente, Andre, and Joost Breuker (1996). "A Functional Ontology of Law," Artificial Intelligence and Law.

51. Waltl, Bernhard, and Roland Vogl (2018). "Explainable Artificial Intelligence: The New Frontier in Legal Informatics," February 2018, Jusletter IT 22, Stanford Center for Legal Informatics, Stanford University.

52. Wittgenstein, Ludwig (1953). Philosophical Investigations. Blackwell Publishing.

APPENDIX B
SUPPLEMENTAL FIGURES AND CHARTS

For the convenience of viewing, supplemental figures and charts related to the topics discussed are shown on the next pages

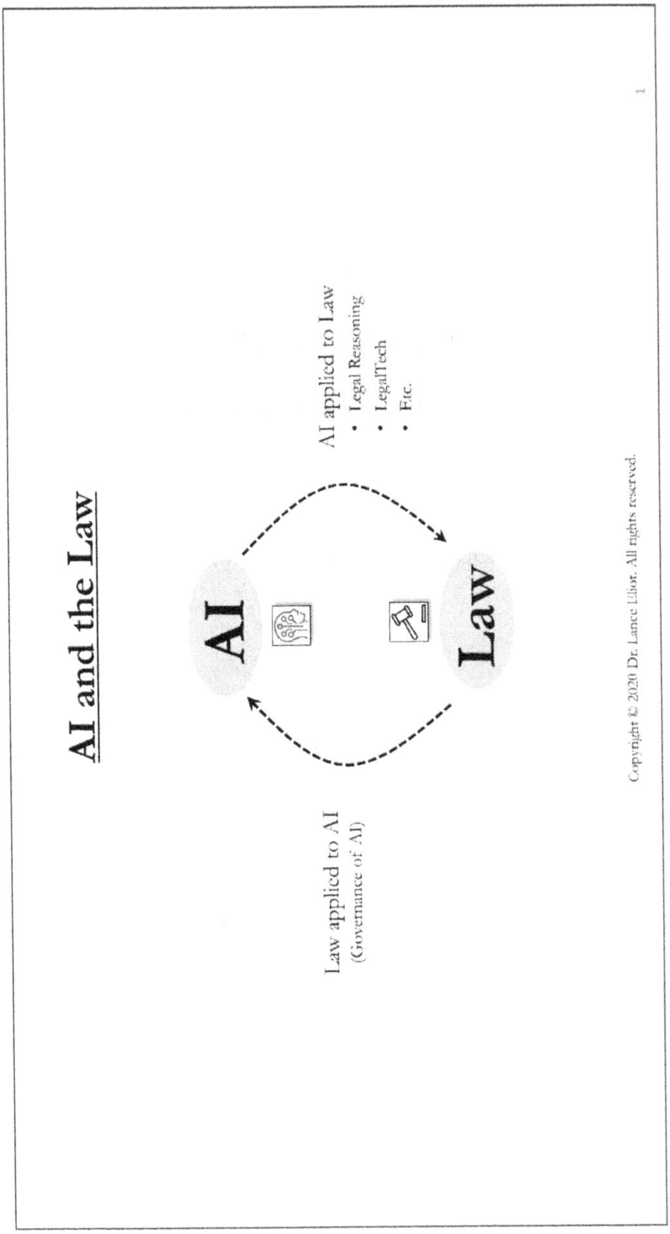
AI and the Law
AI
Law
AI applied to Law
• Legal Reasoning
• LegalTech
• Etc.
Law applied to AI
(Governance of AI)
Copyright © 2020 Dr. Lance Eliot. All rights reserved.
1

Figure 1

AI & Law: Levels of Autonomy For AI Legal Reasoning (AILR)

Level	Descriptor	Examples	Automation	Status
0	No Automation	Manual, paper-based (no automation)	None	De Facto - In Use
1	Simple Assistance Automation	Word Processing, XLS, online legal docs, etc.	Legal Assist	Widely In Use
2	Advanced Assistance Automation	Query-style NLP, ML for case prediction, etc.	Legal Assist	Some In Use
3	Semi-Autonomous Automation	KBS & ML/DL for legal reasoning & analysis, etc.	Legal Assist	Primarily Prototypes & Research Based
4	AILR Domain Autonomous	Versed only in a specific legal domain	Legal Advisor (law fluent)	None As Yet
5	AILR Fully Autonomous	Versatile within and across all legal domains	Legal Advisor (law fluent)	None As Yet
6	AILR Superhuman Autonomous	Exceeds human-based legal reasoning	Supra Legal Advisor	Indeterminate

Figure 1: AI & Law - Autonomous Levels by Rows

Source Author: Dr. Lance B. Eliot

V1.3

Figure 2

AI & Law: Levels of Autonomy For AI Legal Reasoning (AILR)

	Level 0	Level 1	Level 2	Level 3	Level 4	Level 5	Level 6
Descriptor	No Automation	Simple Assistance Automation	Advanced Assistance Automation	Semi-Autonomous Automation	AILR Domain Autonomous	AILR Fully Autonomous	AILR Superhuman Autonomous
Examples	Manual, paper-based (no automation)	Word Processing, XLS, online legal docs, etc.	Query-style NLP, ML for case prediction, etc.	KBS & ML/DL for legal reasoning & analysis, etc.	Versed only in a specific legal domain	Versatile within and across all legal domains	Exceeds human-based legal reasoning
Automation	None	Legal Assist	Legal Assist	Legal Assist	Legal Advisor (law fluent)	Legal Advisor (law fluent)	Supra Legal Advisor
Status	De Facto – In Use	Widely In Use	Some In Use	Primarily Prototypes & Research-based	None As Yet	None As Yet	Indeterminate

Figure 2: AI & Law - Autonomous Levels by Columns

Source Author: Dr. Lance B. Eliot

V1.3

Figure 3

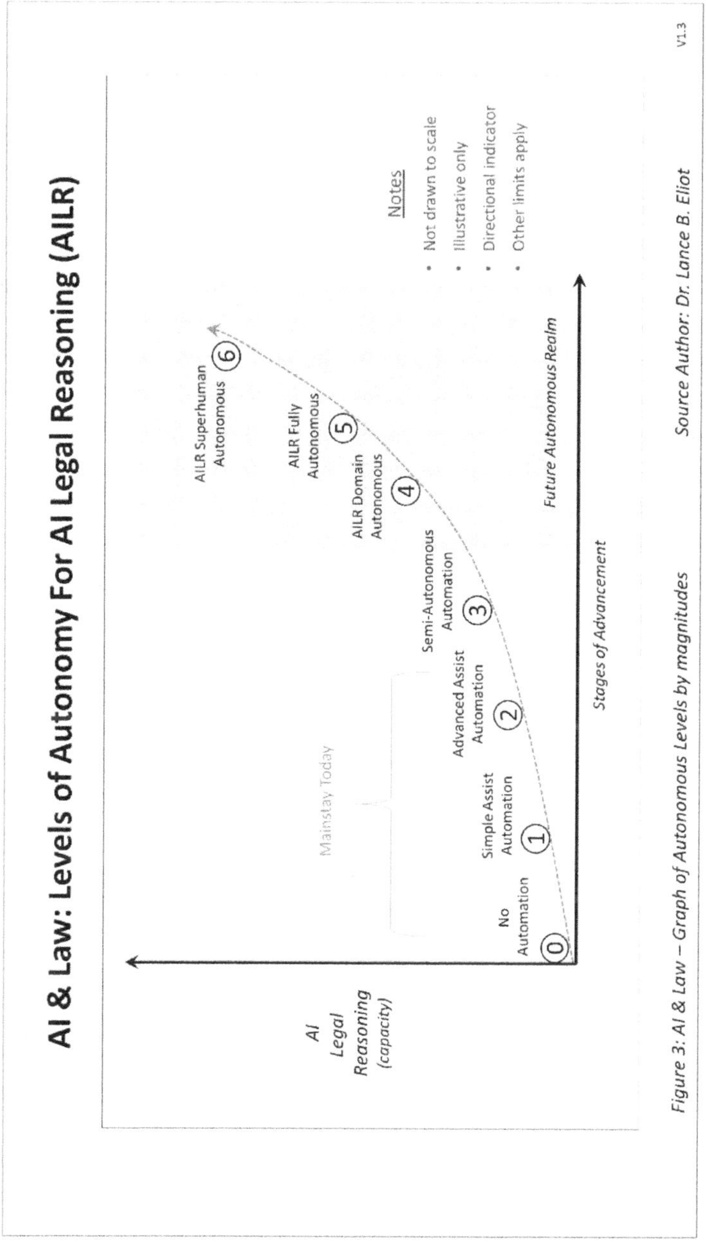
AI & Law: Levels of Autonomy For AI Legal Reasoning (AILR)
AI Legal Reasoning (capacity)
Stages of Advancement
Future Autonomous Realm
Mainstay Today
0 No Automation
1 Simple Assist Automation
2 Advanced Assist Automation
3 Semi-Autonomous Automation
4 AILR Domain Autonomous
5 AILR Fully Autonomous
6 AILR Superhuman Autonomous
Notes
Not drawn to scale
Illustrative only
Directional indicator
Other limits apply
Figure 3: AI & Law – Graph of Autonomous Levels by magnitudes
Source Author: Dr. Lance B. Eliot
V1.3

Figure 4

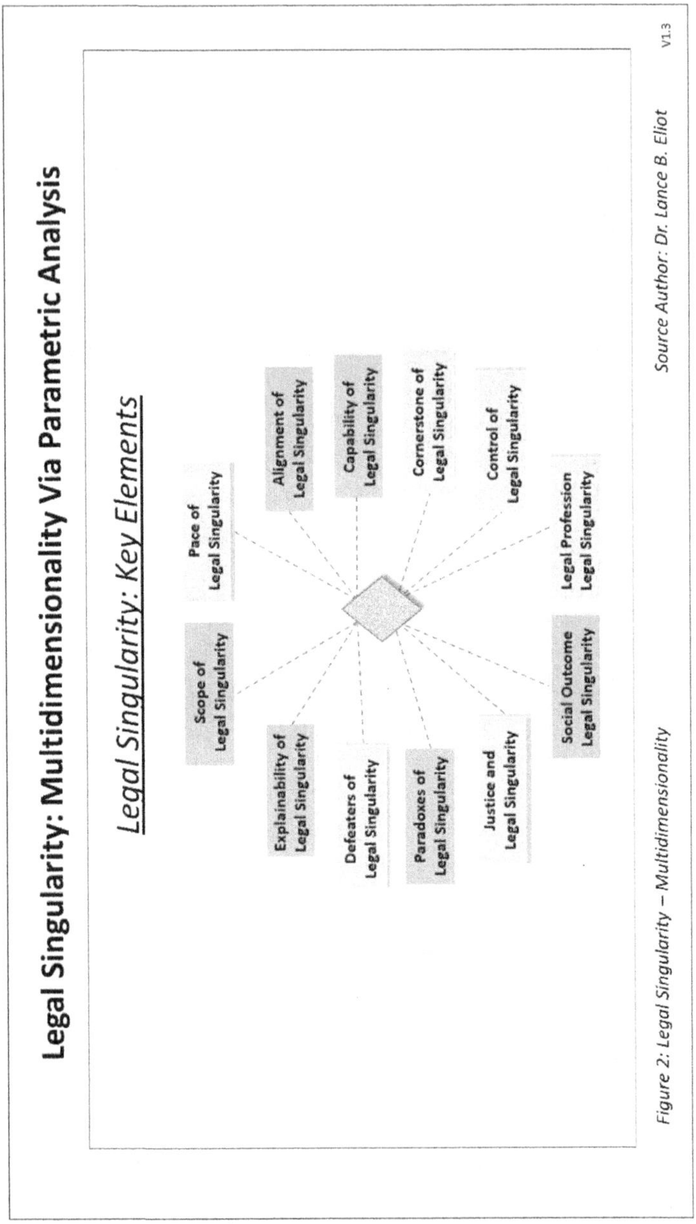
Legal Singularity: Multidimensionality Via Parametric Analysis
Legal Singularity: Key Elements
Scope of Legal Singularity
Pace of Legal Singularity
Alignment of Legal Singularity
Capability of Legal Singularity
Cornerstone of Legal Singularity
Control of Legal Singularity
Legal Profession Legal Singularity
Social Outcome Legal Singularity
Justice and Legal Singularity
Paradoxes of Legal Singularity
Defeaters of Legal Singularity
Explainability of Legal Singularity
Figure 2: Legal Singularity – Multidimensionality
Source Author: Dr. Lance B. Eliot
V1.3

Figure 5

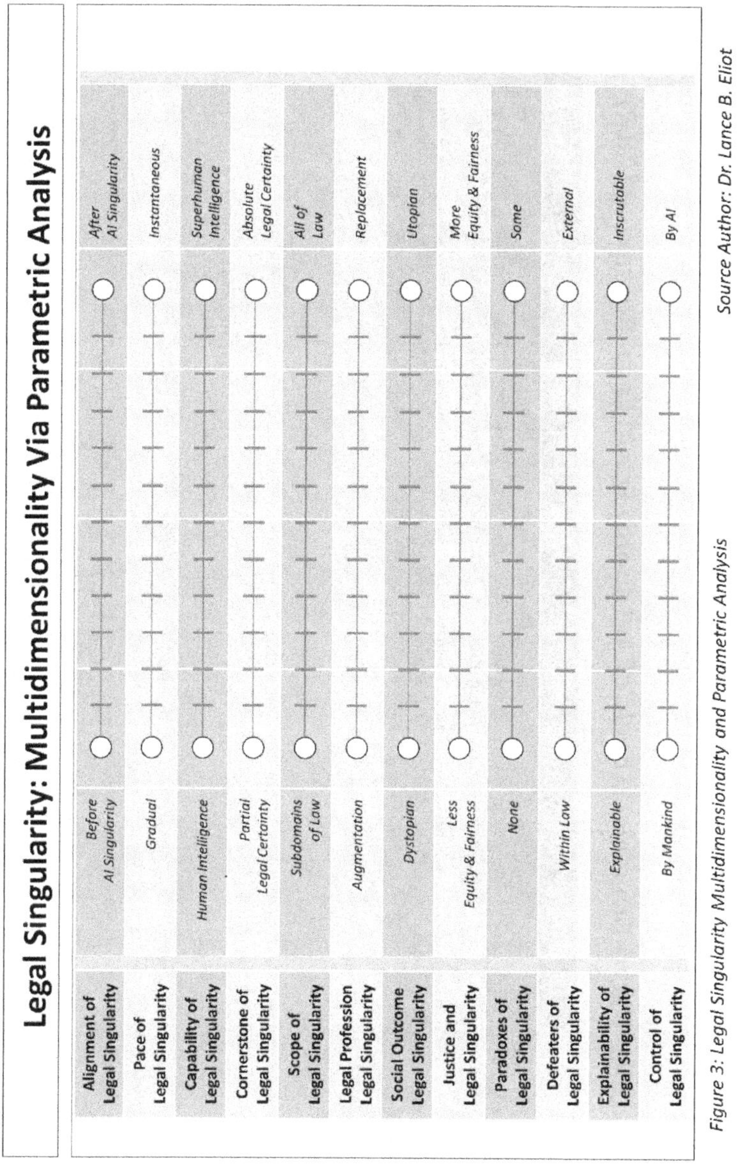
Legal Singularity: Multidimensionality Via Parametric Analysis
Alignment of Legal Singularity
Before AI Singularity
After AI Singularity
Pace of Legal Singularity
Gradual
Instantaneous
Capability of Legal Singularity
Human Intelligence
Superhuman Intelligence
Cornerstone of Legal Singularity
Partial Legal Certainty
Absolute Legal Certainty
Scope of Legal Singularity
Subdomains of Law
All of Law
Legal Profession Legal Singularity
Augmentation
Replacement
Social Outcome Legal Singularity
Dystopian
Utopian
Justice and Legal Singularity
Less Equity & Fairness
More Equity & Fairness
Paradoxes of Legal Singularity
None
Some
Defeaters of Legal Singularity
Within Law
External
Explainability of Legal Singularity
Explainable
Inscrutable
Control of Legal Singularity
By Mankind
By AI
Figure 3: Legal Singularity Multidimensionality and Parametric Analysis
Source Author: Dr. Lance B. Eliot

Figure 6

Legal Micro-Directives: Levels of Autonomy For AI Legal Reasoning (AILR)

	Level 0	Level 1	Level 2	Level 3	Level 4	Level 5	Level 6
Descriptor	No Automation	Simple Assistance Automation	Advanced Assistance Automation	Semi-Autonomous Automation	AILR Domain Autonomous	AILR Fully Autonomous	AILR Superhuman Autonomous
Examples	Manual, paper-based (no automation)	Word Processing, XLS, online legal docs, etc.	Query-style NLP, ML for case prediction, etc.	KBS & ML/DL for legal reasoning & analysis, etc.	Versed only in a specific legal domain	Versatile within and across all legal domains	Exceeds human-based legal reasoning
Automation	None	Legal Assist	Legal Assist	Legal Assist	Legal Advisor (law fluent)	Legal Advisor (law fluent)	Supra Legal Advisor
Status	De Facto – In Use	Widely In Use	Some In Use	Primarily Prototypes & Research-based	None As Yet	None As Yet	Indeterminate
AI-Enabled Legal Micro-Directives	*n/a*	*Impractical*	*Incubatory*	*Infancy*	*Narrow*	*Wide*	*Consummate*

Figure 1: Legal Micro-Directives - Autonomous Levels of AILR by Columns

Source Author: Dr. Lance B. Eliot

V1.3

Figure 7

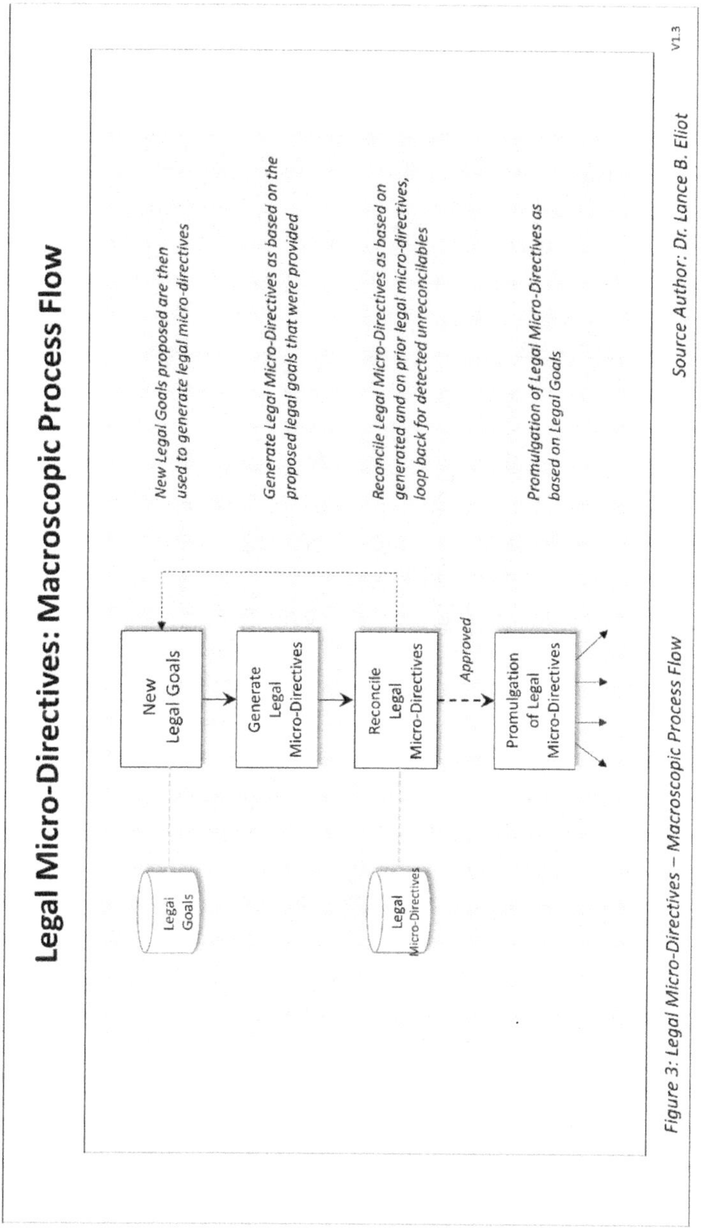
Legal Micro-Directives: Macroscopic Process Flow
Legal Goals
Legal Micro-Directives
New Legal Goals
Generate Legal Micro-Directives
Reconcile Legal Micro-Directives
Approved
Promulgation of Legal Micro-Directives
New Legal Goals proposed are then used to generate legal micro-directives
Generate Legal Micro-Directives as based on the proposed legal goals that were provided
Reconcile Legal Micro-Directives as based on generated and on prior legal micro-directives, loop back for detected unreconcilables
Promulgation of Legal Micro-Directives as based on Legal Goals
Figure 3: Legal Micro-Directives – Macroscopic Process Flow
Source Author: Dr. Lance B. Eliot
V1.3

Figure 8

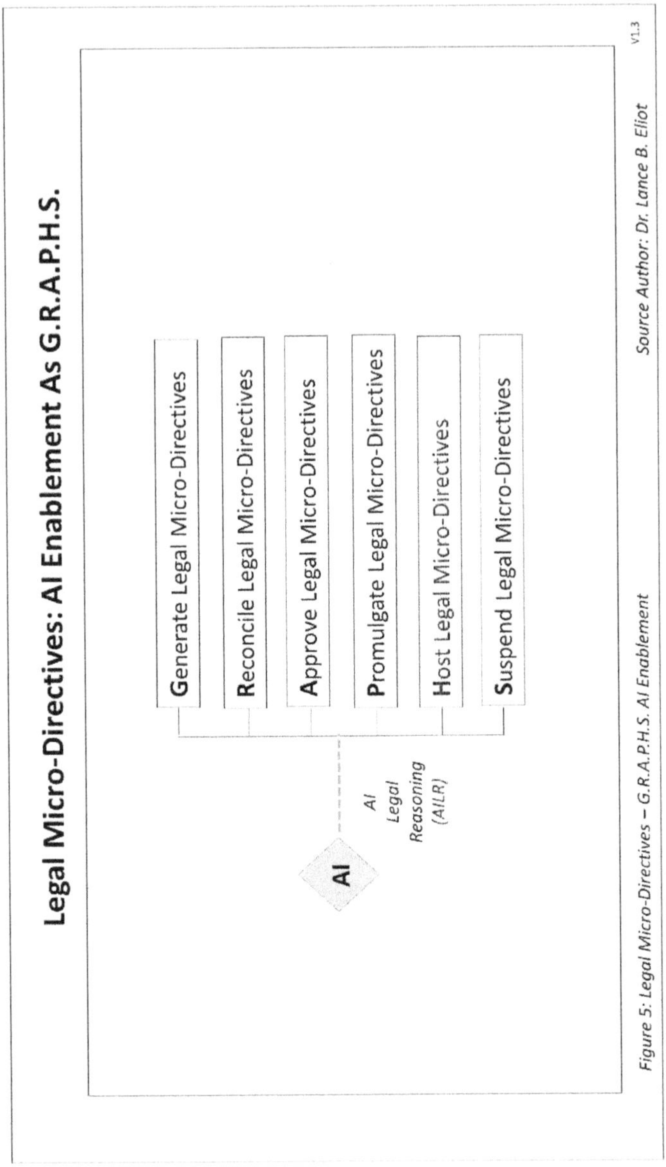
Legal Micro-Directives: AI Enablement As G.R.A.P.H.S.
AI
AI Legal Reasoning (AILR)
Generate Legal Micro-Directives
Reconcile Legal Micro-Directives
Approve Legal Micro-Directives
Promulgate Legal Micro-Directives
Host Legal Micro-Directives
Suspend Legal Micro-Directives
Figure 5: Legal Micro-Directives – G.R.A.P.H.S. AI Enablement
Source Author: Dr. Lance B. Eliot
V1.3

Figure 9

Legal Argumentation: Levels of Autonomy For AI Legal Reasoning (AILR)

	Level 0	Level 1	Level 2	Level 3	Level 4	Level 5	Level 6
Descriptor	No Automation	Simple Assistance Automation	Advanced Assistance Automation	Semi-Autonomous Automation	AILR Domain Autonomous	AILR Fully Autonomous	AILR Superhuman Autonomous
Examples	Manual, paper-based (no automation)	Word Processing, XLS, online legal docs, etc.	Query-style NLP, ML for case prediction, etc.	KBS & ML/DL for legal reasoning & analysis, etc.	Versed only in a specific legal domain	Versatile within and across all legal domains	Exceeds human-based legal reasoning
Automation	None	Legal Assist	Legal Assist	Legal Assist	Legal Advisor (law fluent)	Legal Advisor (law fluent)	Supra Legal Advisor
Status	De Facto – In Use	Widely In Use	Some In Use	Primarily Prototypes & Research-based	None As Yet	None As Yet	Indeterminate
AI-Enabled Legal Argumentation	*n/a*	*Mechanistic (Low)*	*Mechanistic (High)*	*Expressive*	*Domain Fluency*	*Full Fluency*	*Meta-Fluency*

Figure 7: AI Legal Argumentation (AILA) - Autonomous Levels of AILR by Columns *Source Author: Dr. Lance B. Eliot*

V1.3

Figure 10

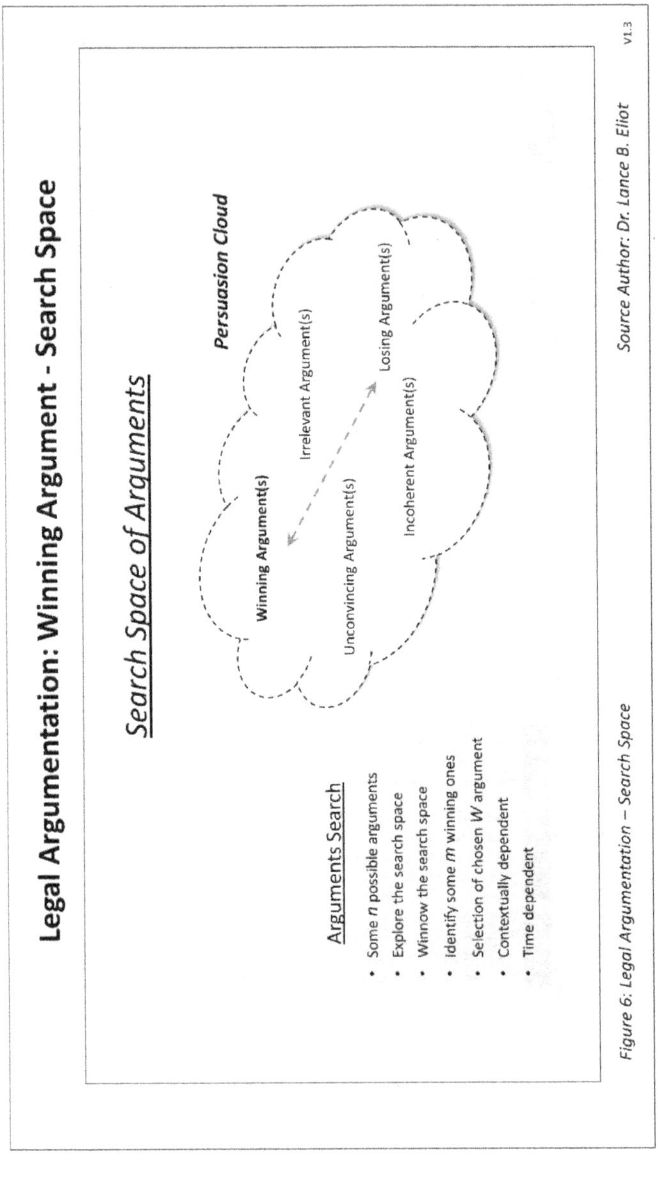
Legal Argumentation: Winning Argument - Search Space
Search Space of Arguments
Persuasion Cloud
Winning Argument(s)
Irrelevant Argument(s)
Losing Argument(s)
Unconvincing Argument(s)
Incoherent Argument(s)
Arguments Search
• Some n possible arguments
• Explore the search space
• Winnow the search space
• Identify some m winning ones
• Selection of chosen W argument
• Contextually dependent
• Time dependent
Figure 6: Legal Argumentation – Search Space
Source Author: Dr. Lance B. Eliot
V1.3

Figure 11

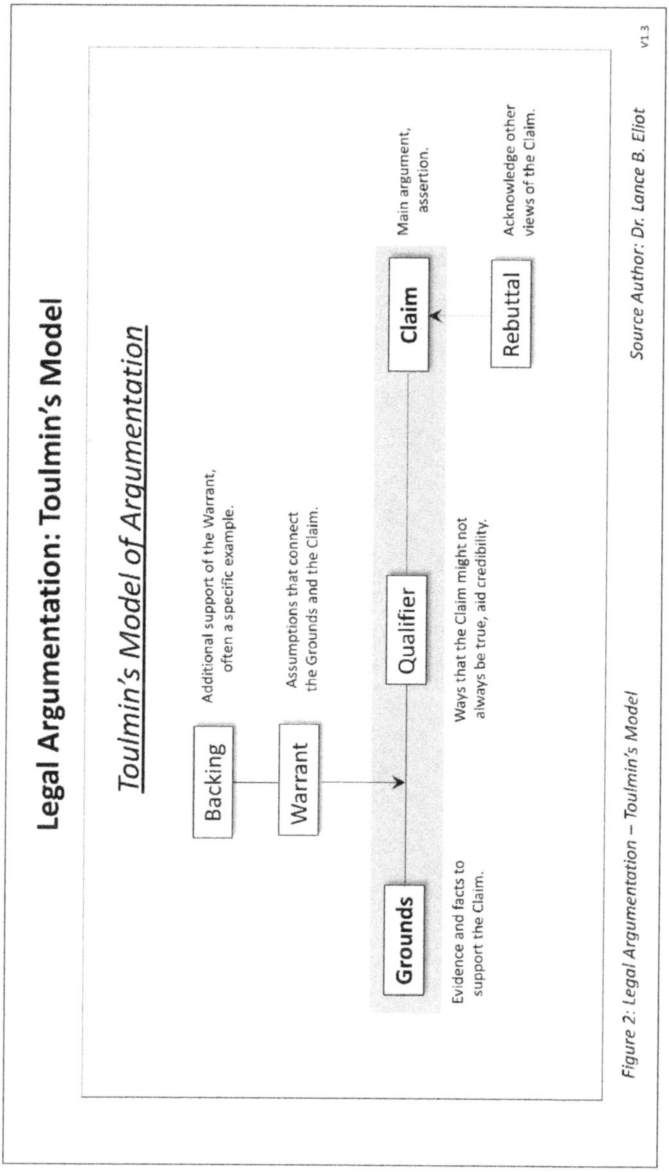
Legal Argumentation: Toulmin's Model
Toulmin's Model of Argumentation
Backing
Additional support of the Warrant, often a specific example.
Warrant
Assumptions that connect the Grounds and the Claim.
Grounds
Evidence and facts to support the Claim.
Qualifier
Ways that the Claim might not always be true, aid credibility.
Claim
Main argument, assertion.
Rebuttal
Acknowledge other views of the Claim.
Figure 2: Legal Argumentation – Toulmin's Model
Source Author: Dr. Lance B. Eliot
V1.3

Figure 12

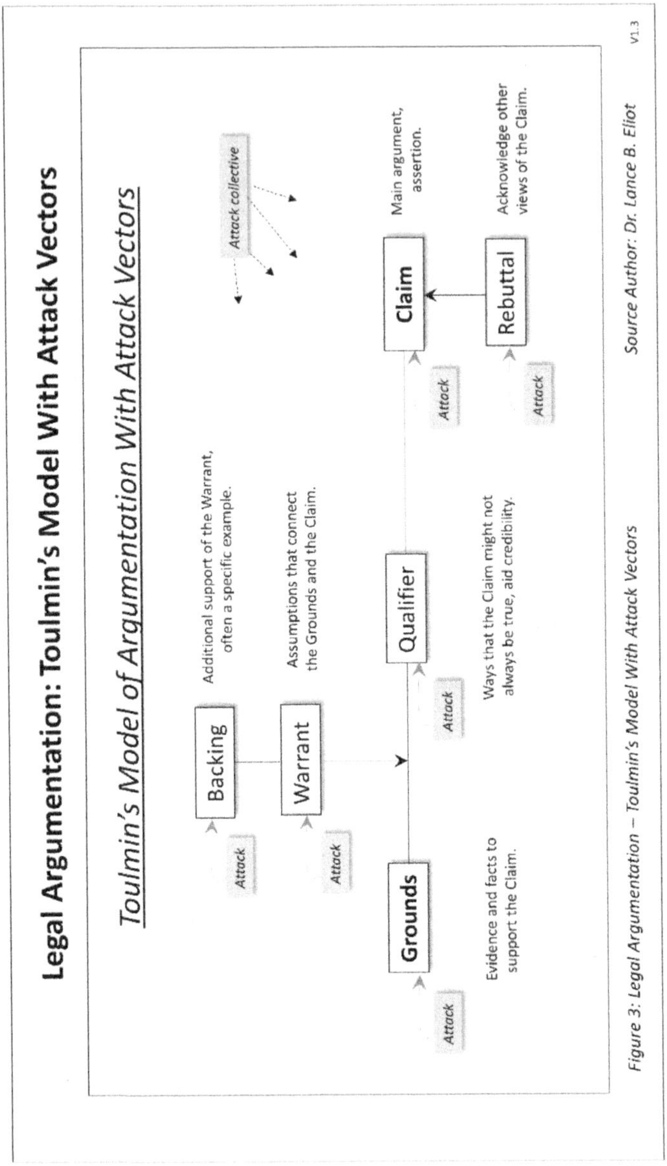
Legal Argumentation: Toulmin's Model With Attack Vectors
Toulmin's Model of Argumentation With Attack Vectors
Backing
Additional support of the Warrant, often a specific example.
Warrant
Assumptions that connect the Grounds and the Claim.
Grounds
Evidence and facts to support the Claim.
Qualifier
Ways that the Claim might not always be true, aid credibility.
Claim
Main argument, assertion.
Rebuttal
Acknowledge other views of the Claim.
Attack
Attack
Attack
Attack
Attack
Attack
Attack collective
Figure 3: Legal Argumentation – Toulmin's Model With Attack Vectors
Source Author: Dr. Lance B. Eliot
V1.3

Figure 13

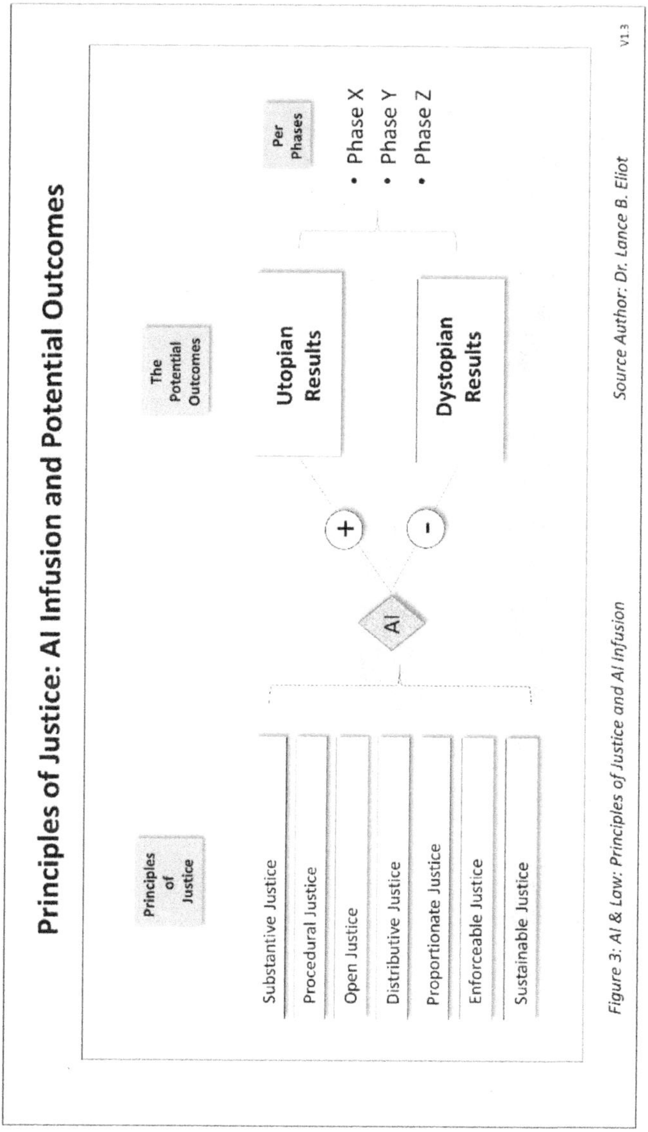
Principles of Justice: AI Infusion and Potential Outcomes
Principles of Justice
Substantive Justice
Procedural Justice
Open Justice
Distributive Justice
Proportionate Justice
Enforceable Justice
Sustainable Justice
AI
+
-
The Potential Outcomes
Utopian Results
Dystopian Results
Per Phases
• Phase X
• Phase Y
• Phase Z
Figure 3: AI & Law: Principles of Justice and AI Infusion
Source Author: Dr. Lance B. Eliot
V1.3

Figure 14

Principles of Justice and Autonomous Levels of AI Legal Reasoning (AILR)

	Level 0	Level 1	Level 2	Level 3	Level 4	Level 5	Level 6
Descriptor	No Automation	Simple Assistance Automation	Advanced Assistance Automation	Semi-Autonomous Automation	AILR Domain Autonomous	AILR Fully Autonomous	AILR Superhuman Autonomous
Substantive Justice	*Traditional*	*Traditional*	*Traditional*	Emerging	Phase X Impacts	Phase Y Impacts	Phase Z Impacts
Procedural Justice	*Traditional*	*Traditional*	*Traditional*	Emerging	Phase X Impacts	Phase Y Impacts	Phase Z Impacts
Open Justice	*Traditional*	*Traditional*	*Traditional*	Emerging	Phase X Impacts	Phase Y Impacts	Phase Z Impacts
Distributive Justice	*Traditional*	*Traditional*	*Traditional*	Emerging	Phase X Impacts	Phase Y Impacts	Phase Z Impacts
Proportionate Justice	*Traditional*	*Traditional*	*Traditional*	Emerging	Phase X Impacts	Phase Y Impacts	Phase Z Impacts
Enforceable Justice	*Traditional*	*Traditional*	*Traditional*	Emerging	Phase X Impacts	Phase Y Impacts	Phase Z Impacts
Sustainable Justice	*Traditional*	*Traditional*	*Traditional*	Emerging	Phase X Impacts	Phase Y Impacts	Phase Z Impacts

Figure 1: AI & Law – Principles of Justice and LoA AILR by Columns

Source Author: Dr. Lance B. Eliot

V1.3

Figure 15

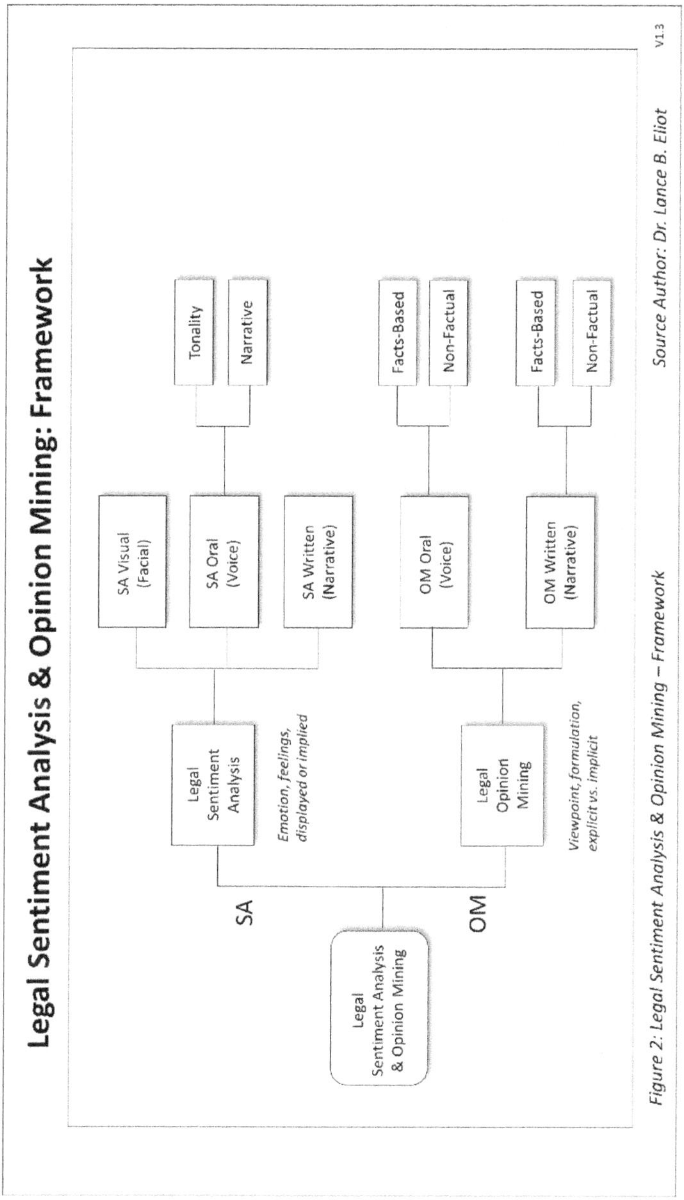
Legal Sentiment Analysis & Opinion Mining: Framework
Legal Sentiment Analysis & Opinion Mining
SA
OM
Legal Sentiment Analysis
Emotion, feelings, displayed or implied
Legal Opinion Mining
Viewpoint, formulation, explicit vs. implicit
SA Visual (Facial)
SA Oral (Voice)
SA Written (Narrative)
OM Oral (Voice)
OM Written (Narrative)
Tonality
Narrative
Facts-Based
Non-Factual
Facts-Based
Non-Factual
Figure 2: Legal Sentiment Analysis & Opinion Mining – Framework
Source Author: Dr. Lance B. Eliot
V1.3

Figure 16

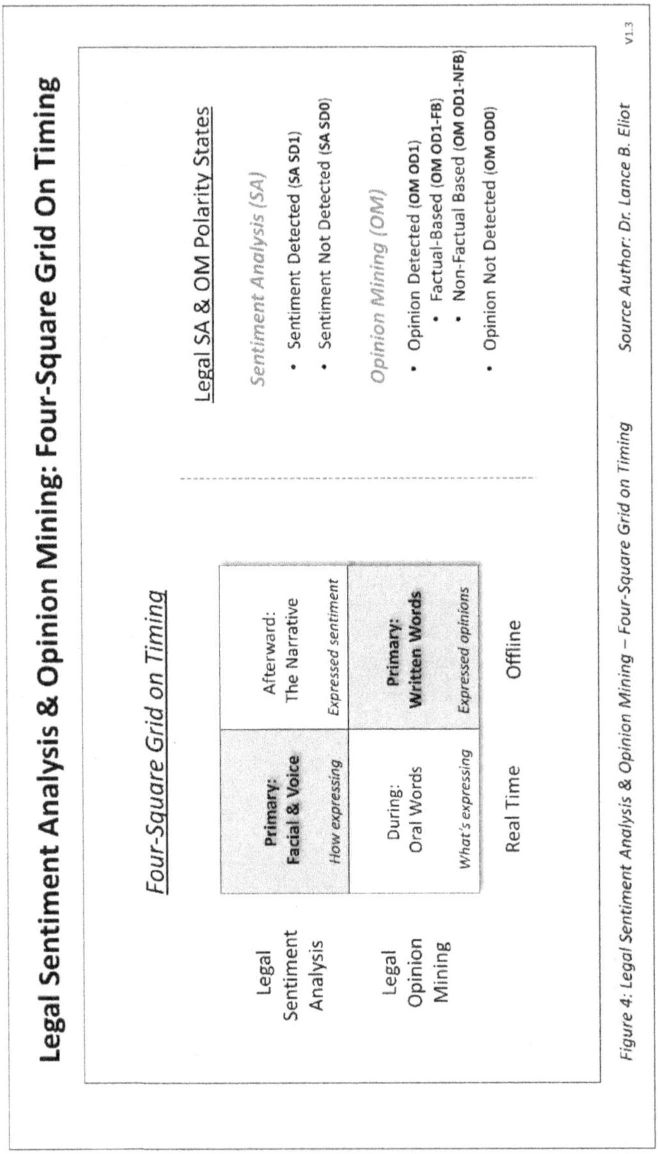
Legal Sentiment Analysis & Opinion Mining: Four-Square Grid On Timing
Four-Square Grid on Timing
Legal Sentiment Analysis
Legal Opinion Mining
Primary: Facial & Voice
How expressing
Afterward: The Narrative
Expressed sentiment
During: Oral Words
What's expressing
Primary: Written Words
Expressed opinions
Real Time
Offline
Legal SA & OM Polarity States
Sentiment Analysis (SA)
Sentiment Detected (SA SD1)
Sentiment Not Detected (SA SD0)
Opinion Mining (OM)
Opinion Detected (OM OD1)
Factual-Based (OM OD1-FB)
Non-Factual Based (OM OD1-NFB)
Opinion Not Detected (OM OD0)
Figure 4: Legal Sentiment Analysis & Opinion Mining – Four-Square Grid on Timing
Source Author: Dr. Lance B. Eliot
V1.3

Figure 17

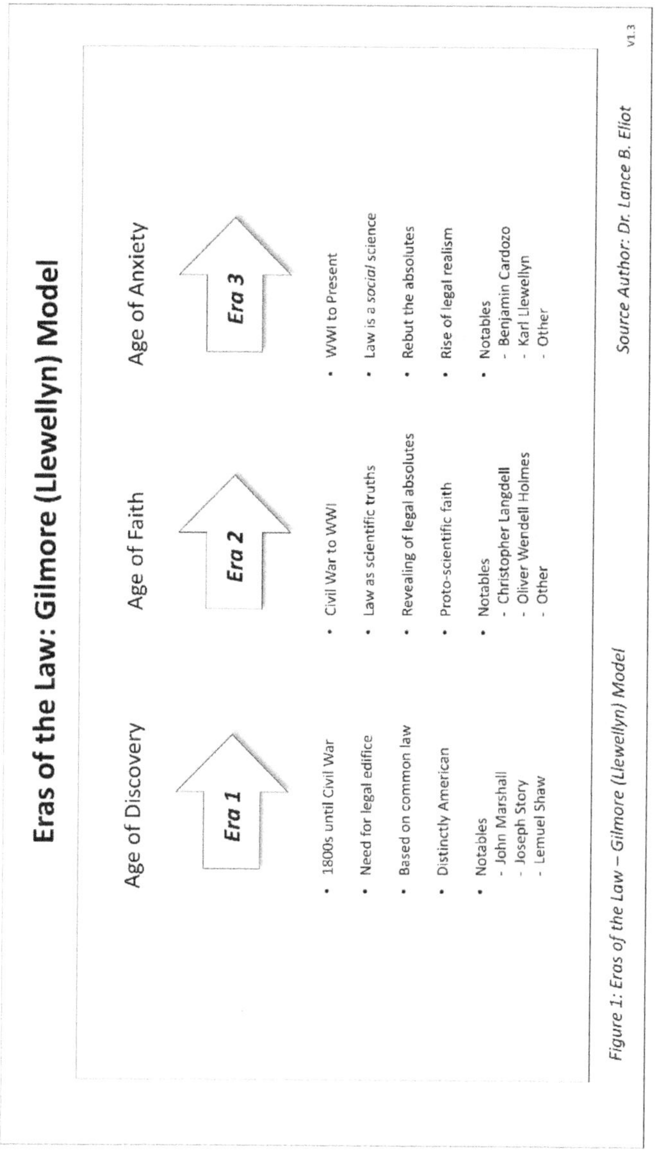
Eras of the Law: Gilmore (Llewellyn) Model
Age of Discovery
Era 1
1800s until Civil War
Need for legal edifice
Based on common law
Distinctly American
Notables
- John Marshall
- Joseph Story
- Lemuel Shaw
Age of Faith
Era 2
Civil War to WWI
Law as scientific truths
Revealing of legal absolutes
Proto-scientific faith
Notables
- Christopher Langdell
- Oliver Wendell Holmes
- Other
Age of Anxiety
Era 3
WWI to Present
Law is a social science
Rebut the absolutes
Rise of legal realism
Notables
- Benjamin Cardozo
- Karl Llewellyn
- Other
Figure 1: Eras of the Law – Gilmore (Llewellyn) Model
Source Author: Dr. Lance B. Eliot
V1.3

Figure 18

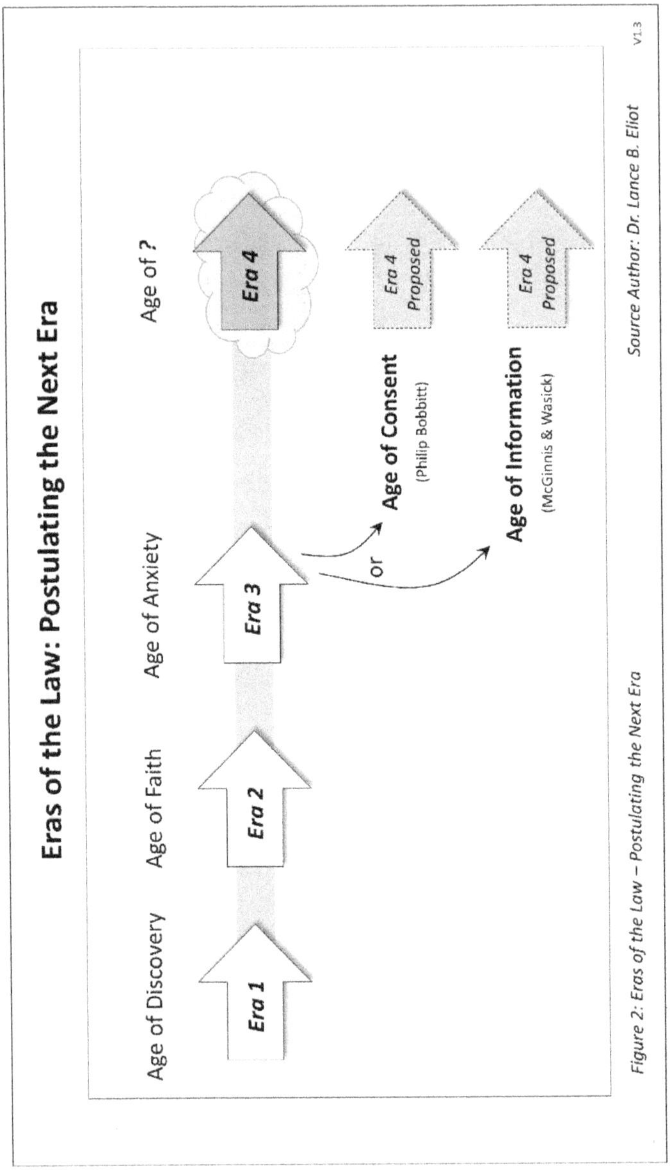
Eras of the Law: Postulating the Next Era
Age of Discovery
Age of Faith
Age of Anxiety
Age of ?
Era 1
Era 2
Era 3
Era 4
or
Age of Consent
(Philip Bobbitt)
Age of Information
(McGinnis & Wasick)
Era 4 Proposed
Era 4 Proposed
Figure 2: Eras of the Law – Postulating the Next Era
Source Author: Dr. Lance B. Eliot
V1.3

Figure 19

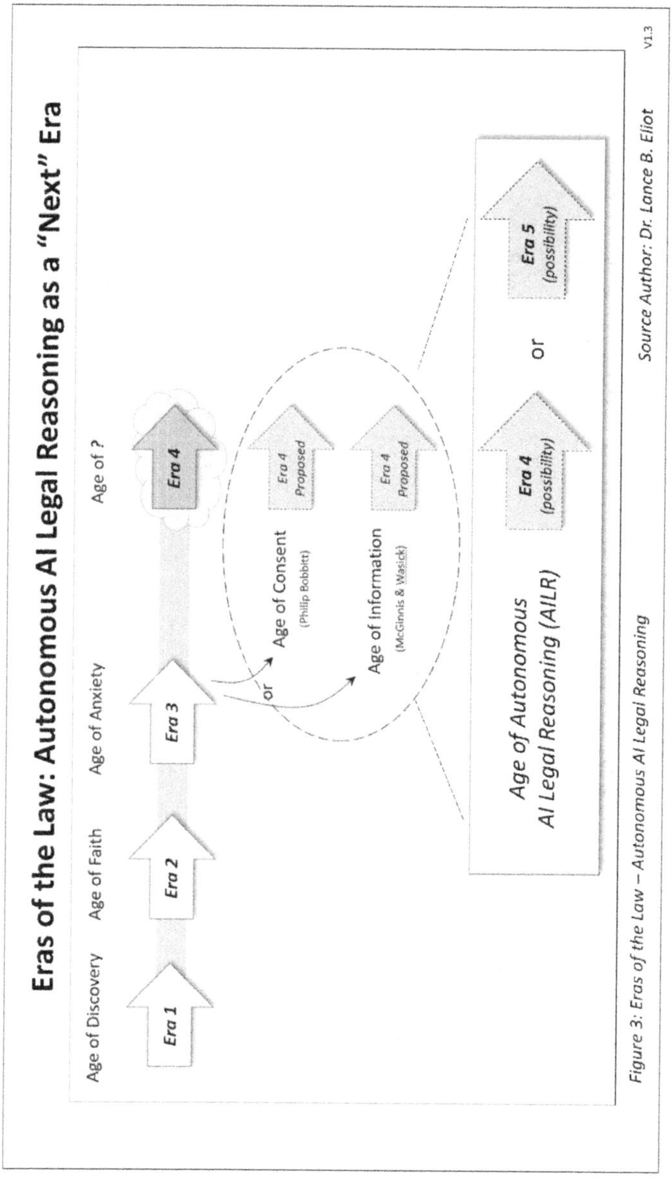
Eras of the Law: Autonomous AI Legal Reasoning as a "Next" Era
Age of Discovery
Age of Faith
Age of Anxiety
Age of ?
Era 1
Era 2
Era 3
Era 4
or
Age of Consent
(Philip Bobbitt)
Age of Information
(McGinnis & Wasick)
Era 4 Proposed
Era 4 Proposed
Age of Autonomous
AI Legal Reasoning (AILR)
Era 4 (possibility)
or
Era 5 (possibility)
Figure 3: Eras of the Law – Autonomous AI Legal Reasoning
Source Author: Dr. Lance B. Eliot
V1.3

Figure 20

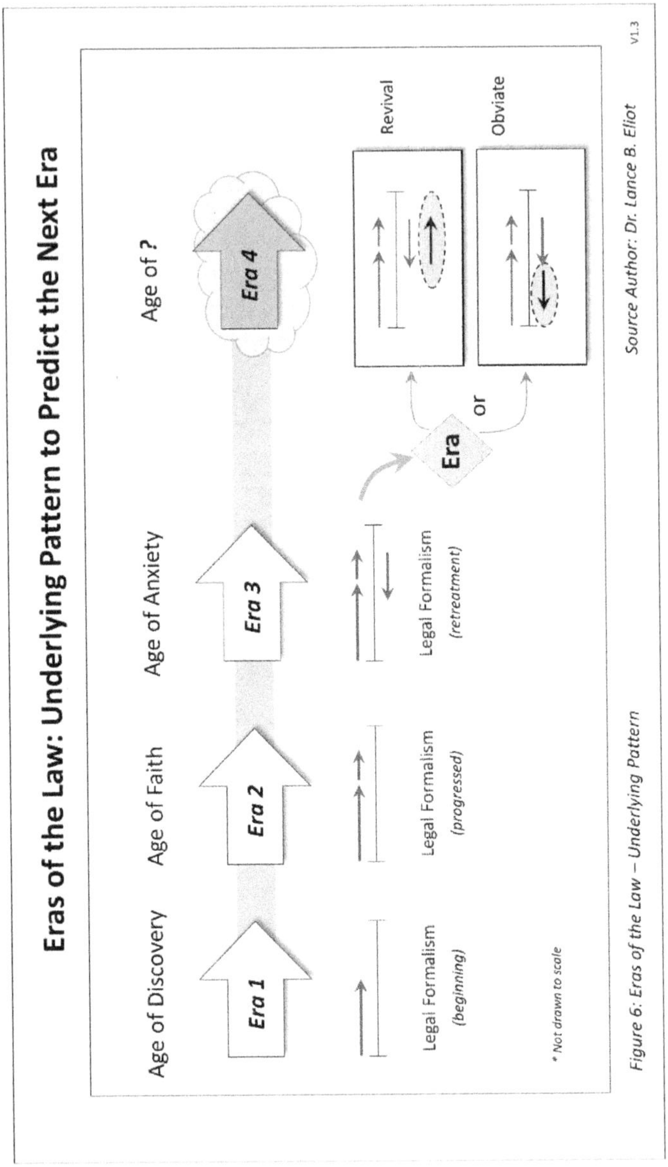
Eras of the Law: Underlying Pattern to Predict the Next Era
Age of Discovery
Age of Faith
Age of Anxiety
Age of ?
Era 1
Era 2
Era 3
Era 4
Legal Formalism
(beginning)
Legal Formalism
(progressed)
Legal Formalism
(retreatment)
Era
or
Revival
Obviate
* Not drawn to scale
Figure 6: Eras of the Law – Underlying Pattern
Source Author: Dr. Lance B. Eliot
V1.3

Figure 21

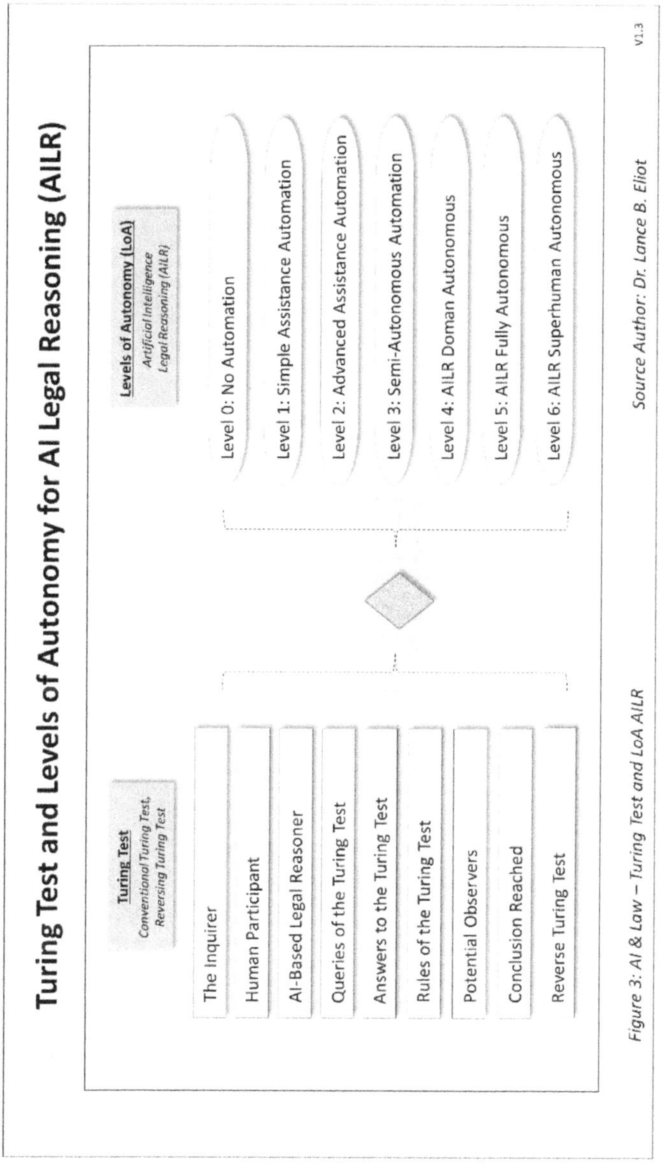
Turing Test and Levels of Autonomy for AI Legal Reasoning (AILR)
Turing Test
Conventional Turing Test,
Reversing Turing Test
Levels of Autonomy (LoA)
Artificial Intelligence
Legal Reasoning (AILR)
The Inquirer
Human Participant
AI-Based Legal Reasoner
Queries of the Turing Test
Answers to the Turing Test
Rules of the Turing Test
Potential Observers
Conclusion Reached
Reverse Turing Test
Level 0: No Automation
Level 1: Simple Assistance Automation
Level 2: Advanced Assistance Automation
Level 3: Semi-Autonomous Automation
Level 4: AILR Doman Autonomous
Level 5: AILR Fully Autonomous
Level 6: AILR Superhuman Autonomous
Figure 3: AI & Law – Turing Test and LoA AILR
Source Author: Dr. Lance B. Eliot
V1.3

Figure 22

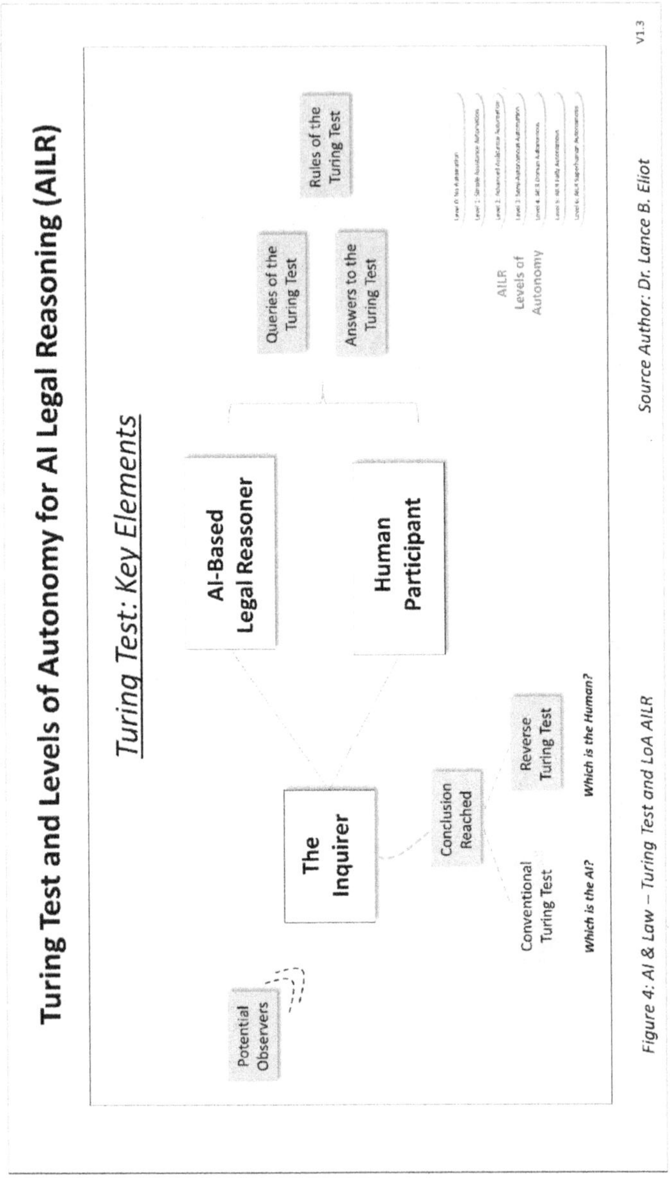
Turing Test and Levels of Autonomy for AI Legal Reasoning (AILR)
Turing Test: Key Elements
Potential Observers
The Inquirer
AI-Based Legal Reasoner
Human Participant
Queries of the Turing Test
Answers to the Turing Test
Rules of the Turing Test
Conclusion Reached
Conventional Turing Test
Reverse Turing Test
Which is the AI?
Which is the Human?
AILR Levels of Autonomy
V1.3
Figure 4: AI & Law – Turing Test and LoA AILR
Source Author: Dr. Lance B. Eliot

Figure 23

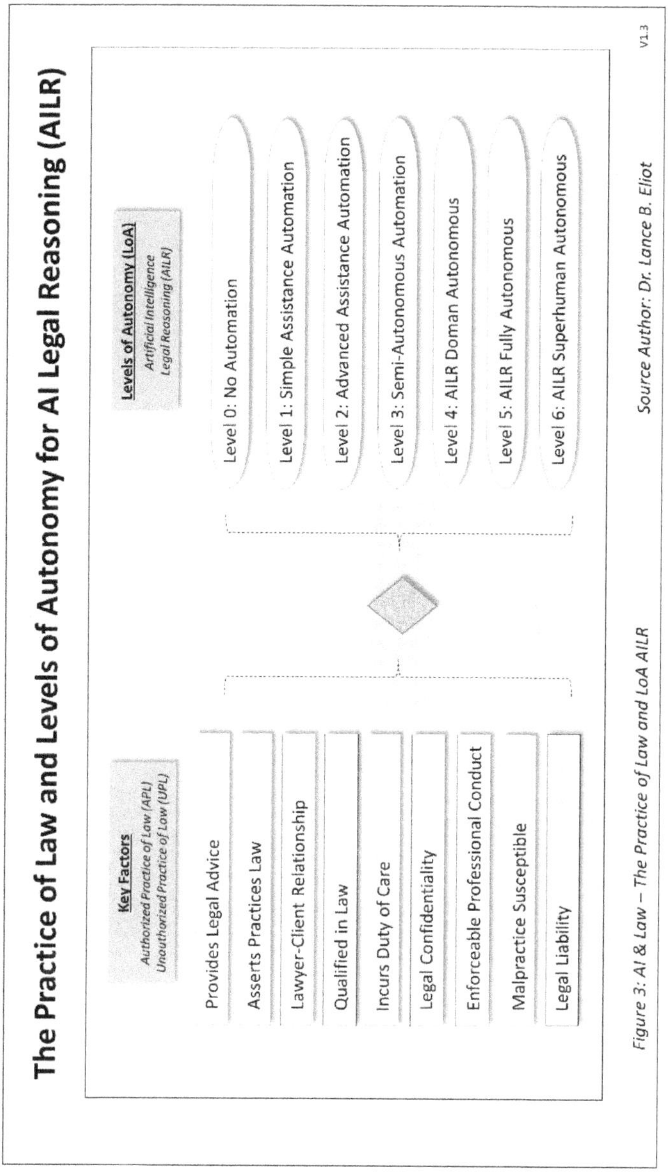

Figure 3: AI & Law – The Practice of Law and LoA AILR

Source Author: Dr. Lance B. Eliot

Figure 24

Strawman Variant

The Practice of Law and Autonomous Levels of AI Legal Reasoning (AILR)

Descriptor	Level 0 No Automation	Level 1 Simple Assistance Automation	Level 2 Advanced Assistance Automation	Level 3 Semi-Autonomous Automation	Level 4 AILR Domain Autonomous	Level 5 AILR Fully Autonomous	Level 6 AILR Superhuman Autonomous
Provides Legal Advice	n/a	No	Maybe	Yes	Yes	Yes	Yes Plus
Asserts Practices Law	n/a	No	No	No	Yes	Yes	Yes Plus
Lawyer-Client Relationship	n/a	No	No	No	Partial	Yes	Yes
Qualified in Law	n/a	No	No	Minimal	Partial	Yes	Yes Plus
Incurs Duty of Care	n/a	No	No	No	Likely	Yes	Yes
Legal Confidentiality	n/a	No	No	No	Likely	Yes	Yes
Enforceable Prof Conduct	n/a	No	No	No	Likely	Yes	Yes
Malpractice Susceptible	n/a	No	No	No	Likely	Yes	Yes
Legal Liability	n/a	No	Maybe	Likely	Likely	Yes	Yes

Figure 1: AI & Law – The Practice of Law and LoA AILR by Columns

Source Author: Dr. Lance B. Eliot

V1.3

Figure 25

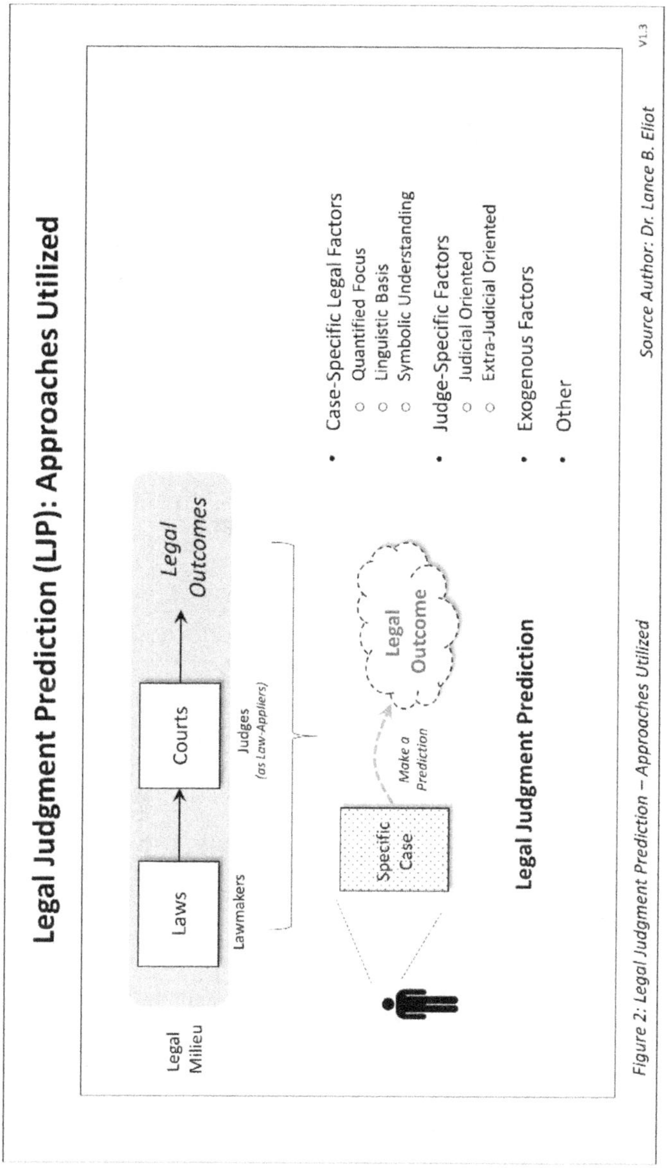
Legal Judgment Prediction (LJP): Approaches Utilized
Legal Milieu
Laws
Courts
Legal Outcomes
Lawmakers
Judges (as Law-Appliers)
Specific Case
Make a Prediction
Legal Outcome
Legal Judgment Prediction
Case-Specific Legal Factors
Quantified Focus
Linguistic Basis
Symbolic Understanding
Judge-Specific Factors
Judicial Oriented
Extra-Judicial Oriented
Exogenous Factors
Other
Figure 2: Legal Judgment Prediction – Approaches Utilized
Source Author: Dr. Lance B. Eliot
V1.3

Figure 26

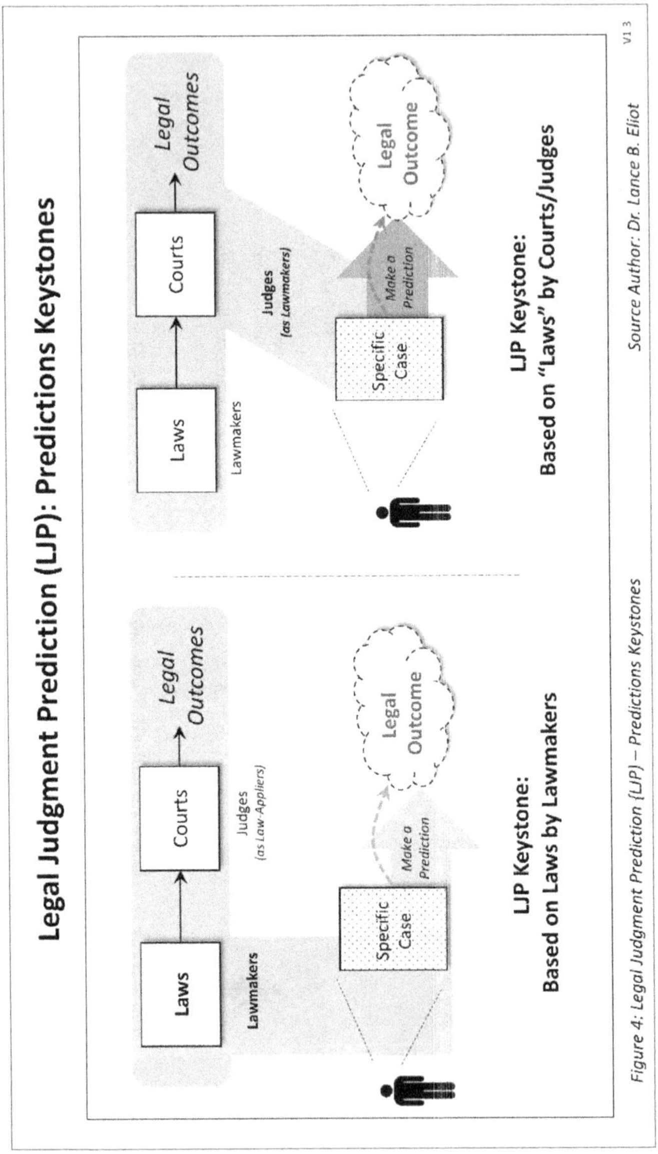
Legal Judgment Prediction (LJP): Predictions Keystones
Laws
Courts
Legal Outcomes
Lawmakers
Judges (as Law-Appliers)
Specific Case
Make a Prediction
Legal Outcome
LJP Keystone: Based on Laws by Lawmakers
Laws
Courts
Legal Outcomes
Lawmakers
Judges (as Lawmakers)
Specific Case
Make a Prediction
Legal Outcome
LJP Keystone: Based on "Laws" by Courts/Judges
Figure 4: Legal Judgment Prediction (LJP) – Predictions Keystones
Source Author: Dr. Lance B. Eliot
V13

Figure 27

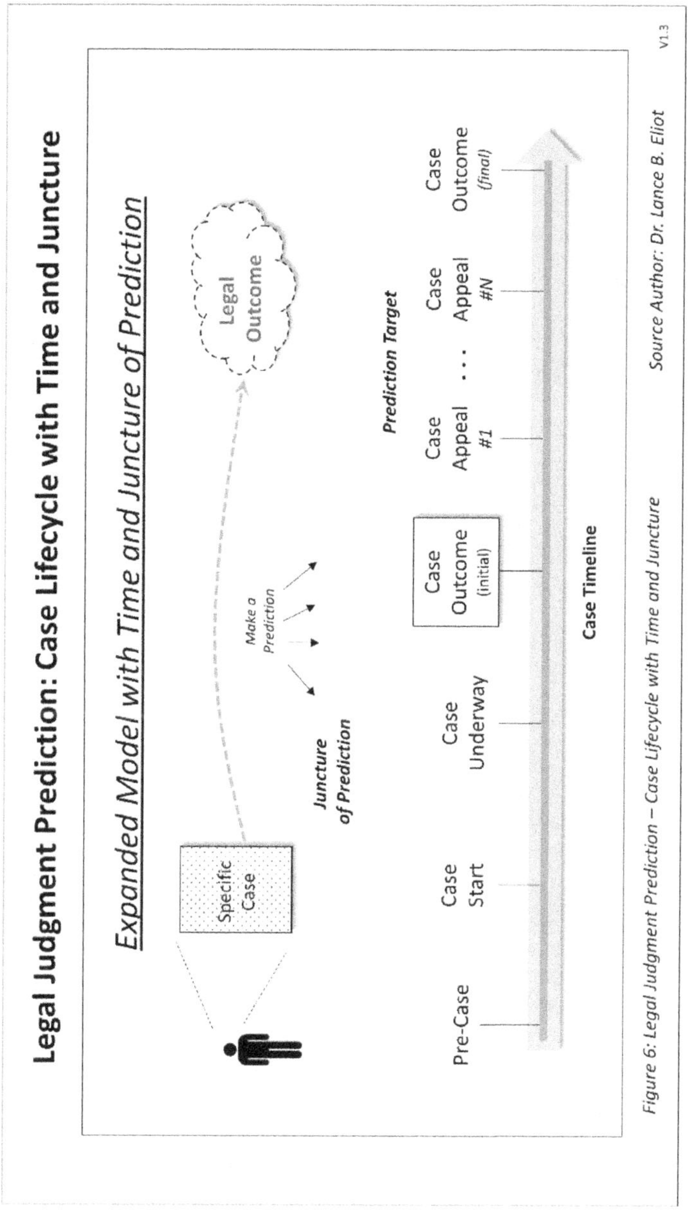
Legal Judgment Prediction: Case Lifecycle with Time and Juncture
Expanded Model with Time and Juncture of Prediction
Specific Case
Legal Outcome
Make a Prediction
Juncture of Prediction
Prediction Target
Pre-Case
Case Start
Case Underway
Case Outcome (initial)
Case Appeal #1
. . .
Case Appeal #N
Case Outcome (final)
Case Timeline
Figure 6: Legal Judgment Prediction – Case Lifecycle with Time and Juncture
Source Author: Dr. Lance B. Eliot
V1.3

Figure 28

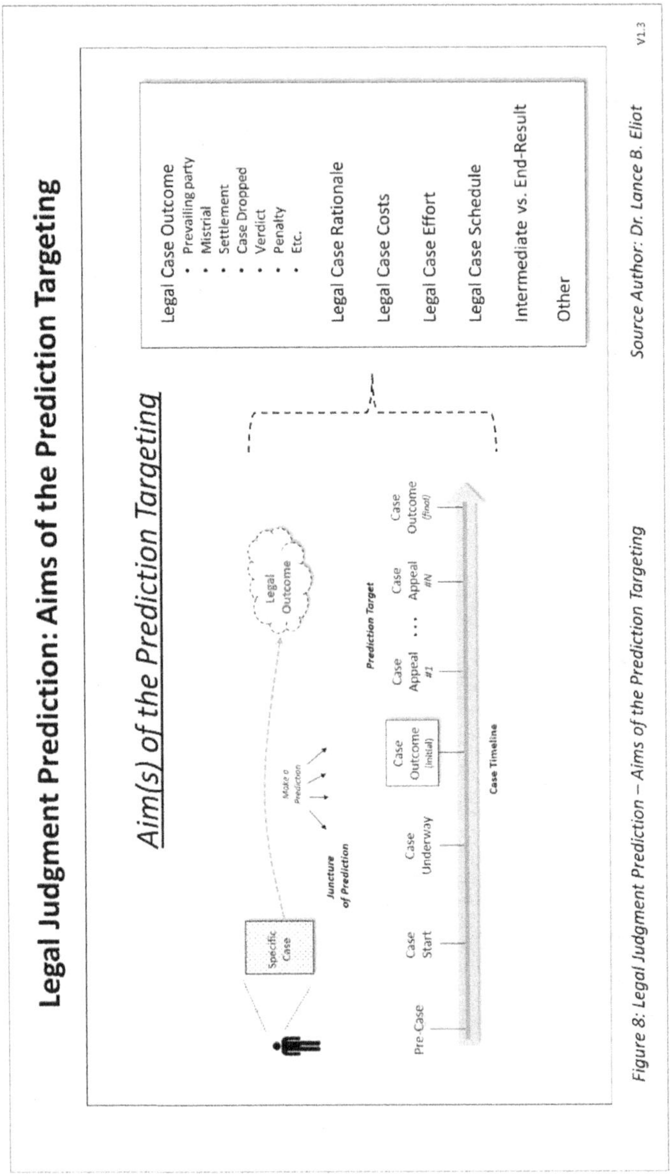
Legal Judgment Prediction: Aims of the Prediction Targeting
Aim(s) of the Prediction Targeting
Specific Case
Juncture of Prediction
Make a Prediction
Legal Outcome
Prediction Target
Pre-Case
Case Start
Case Underway
Case Outcome (initial)
Case Appeal #1
. . .
Case Appeal #N
Case Outcome (final)
Case Timeline
Legal Case Outcome
Prevailing party
Mistrial
Settlement
Case Dropped
Verdict
Penalty
Etc.
Legal Case Rationale
Legal Case Costs
Legal Case Effort
Legal Case Schedule
Intermediate vs. End-Result
Other
Figure 8: Legal Judgment Prediction – Aims of the Prediction Targeting
Source Author: Dr. Lance B. Eliot
V1.3

Figure 29

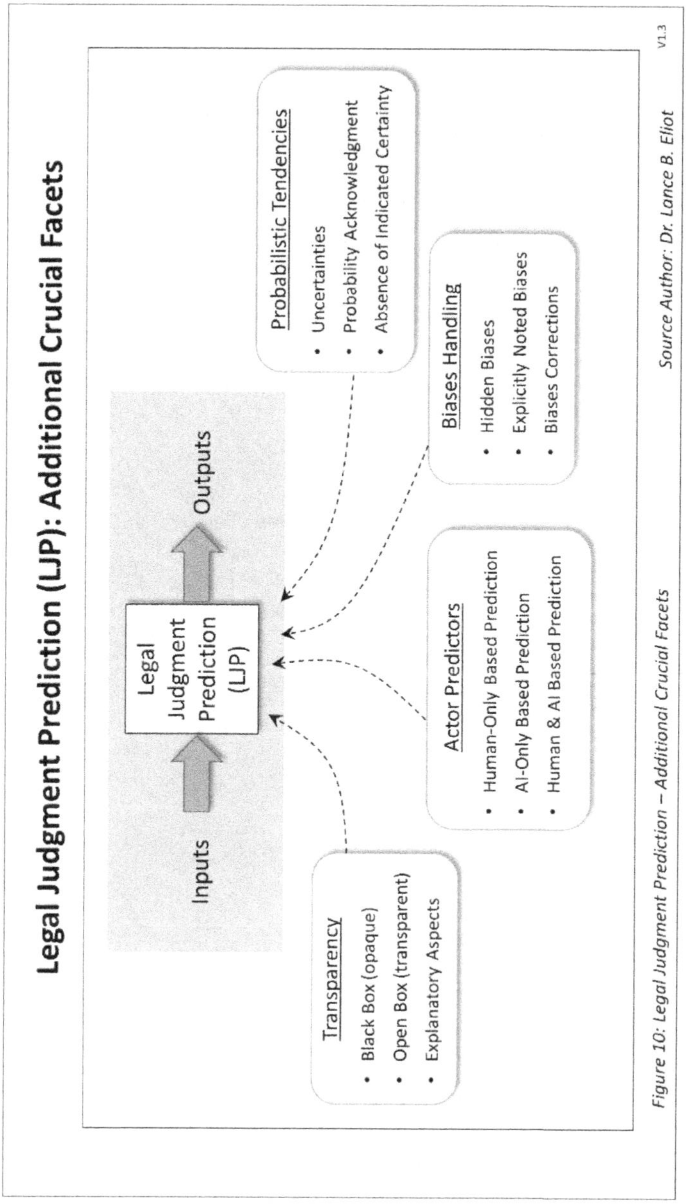
Legal Judgment Prediction (LJP): Additional Crucial Facets
Inputs
Legal Judgment Prediction (LJP)
Outputs
Transparency
Black Box (opaque)
Open Box (transparent)
Explanatory Aspects
Actor Predictors
Human-Only Based Prediction
AI-Only Based Prediction
Human & AI Based Prediction
Biases Handling
Hidden Biases
Explicitly Noted Biases
Biases Corrections
Probabilistic Tendencies
Uncertainties
Probability Acknowledgment
Absence of Indicated Certainty
Figure 10: Legal Judgment Prediction – Additional Crucial Facets
Source Author: Dr. Lance B. Eliot
V1.3

Figure 30

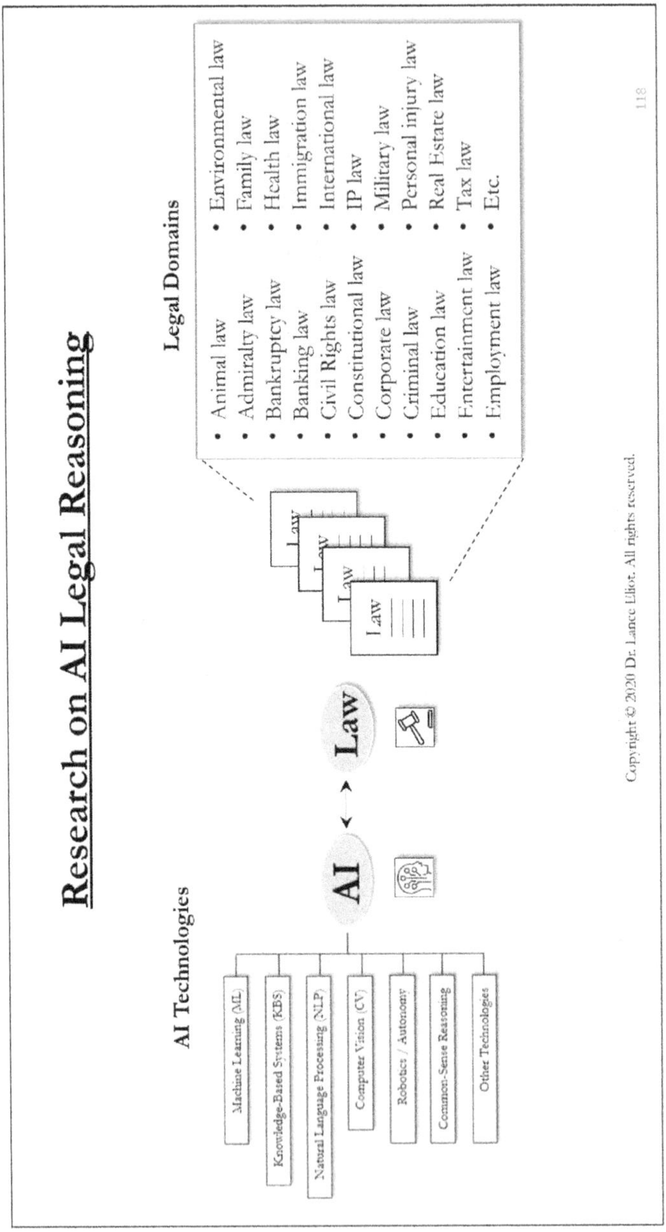

Research on AI Legal Reasoning
AI Technologies
Machine Learning (ML)
Knowledge-Based Systems (KBS)
Natural Language Processing (NLP)
Computer Vision (CV)
Robotics / Autonomy
Common-Sense Reasoning
Other Technologies
AI
Law
Law
Law
Law
Law
Legal Domains
• Animal law
• Admiralty law
• Bankruptcy law
• Banking law
• Civil Rights law
• Constitutional law
• Corporate law
• Criminal law
• Education law
• Entertainment law
• Employment law
• Environmental law
• Family law
• Health law
• Immigration law
• International law
• IP law
• Military law
• Personal injury law
• Real Estate law
• Tax law
• Etc.
Copyright © 2020 Dr. Lance Eliot. All rights reserved.
118

Figure 31

ABOUT THE AUTHOR

Dr. Lance B. Eliot, Ph.D., MBA is a globally recognized AI expert and thought leader, an invited Stanford Fellow at Stanford University, an experienced top executive and corporate leader, a successful entrepreneur, and a noted scholar on AI, including that his Forbes and AI Trends columns have amassed over 4 million views, his books on AI are ranked in the Top 10 of all-time AI books, his journal articles are widely cited, and he has developed and implemented numerous AI systems.

He currently serves as the Chief AI Scientist at Techbruim, Inc. and has over twenty years of industry experience including serving as a corporate officer in billion-dollar sized firms and was a partner in a major consulting firm. He is also a successful entrepreneur having founded, ran, and sold several high-tech related businesses.

Dr. Eliot previously hosted the popular radio show *Technotrends* that was also available on American Airlines flights via their in-flight audio program, he has made appearances on CNN, has been a frequent speaker at industry conferences, and his podcasts have been downloaded over 150,000 times.

A former professor at the University of Southern California (USC), he founded and led an innovative research lab on Artificial Intelligence. He also previously served on the faculty of the University of California Los Angeles (UCLA) and was a visiting professor at other major universities. He was elected to the International Board of the Society for Information Management (SIM), a prestigious association of over 3,000 high-tech executives worldwide.

He has performed extensive community service, including serving as Senior Science Adviser to the Congressional Vice-Chair of the Congressional Committee on Science & Technology. He has served on the Board of the OC Science & Engineering Fair (OCSEF), where he is also has been a Grand Sweepstakes judge, and likewise served as a judge for the Intel International SEF (ISEF). He served as the Vice-Chair of the Association for Computing Machinery (ACM) Chapter, a prestigious association of computer scientists. Dr. Eliot has been a shark tank judge for the USC Mark Stevens Center for Innovation on start-up pitch competitions and served as a mentor for several incubators and accelerators in Silicon Valley and in Silicon Beach.

Dr. Eliot holds a Ph.D. from USC, MBA, and Bachelor's in Computer Science, and earned the CDP, CCP, CSP, CDE, and CISA certification.

Companion Book By Dr. Lance Eliot

"Artificial Intelligence and Legal Reasoning Essentials"

ISBN 978-1-73460165-7

Chapters

01 AI and Law
02 Law is Semantically Indeterminate
03 Misuse of Robo-Lawyer Moniker
04 Defining Legal Reasoning
05 Ontology of Law
06 Intractability of Legal Reasoning
07 AI Black Box and Practicing Law
08 AI Black Box and Being a Lawyer
09 Popov v Hayashi as AI Testbed
10 Non-Monotonic Logic and Legal Reasoning
11 ASPIC+ for Legal Reasoning
12 ASP for Legal Reasoning
13 Meta-Physics of Legal Reasoning
14 Computational Law
15 TAXMAN: AI Case Study
16 HYPO: AI Case Study
17 CATO: AI Case Study
18 SHYSTER: AI Case Study
19 ROSS: AI LegalTech Example
20 Building AI Legal Reasoning Applications
21 Taxonomy of AI Technologies
22 AI Machine Learning
23 Explainability and XAI
24 Legal Implications of AI Legal Reasoning
25 Research Framework of AI Legal Reasoning
Appendices

Available on Amazon and via other online book sellers

Companion Book By Dr. Lance Eliot

"Artificial Intelligence and LegalTech Essentials"

ISBN 978-1-7346016-3-3

Chapters

01 AI And Law

02 LegalTech Versus LawTech

03 Digital Transformation Of Legal Practices

04 Legal Activities Framework

05 AI And LegalTech Building Blocks

06 AI Fundamentals

07 Taxonomy Of AI Technologies

08 AI And LegalTech

09 Case Study: ContractXpert

10 Opportunities For AI LegalTech

11 Keeping Up With AI LegalTech

12 It's A Wrap, Until Tomorrow

Appendix A: Teaching with this Material

Appendix B: Selected Figures and Charts

About the Author

Addendum

Companion Book By Dr. Lance Eliot

"Decisive Essays On AI And Law"

ISBN 978-1-73630310-8

Chapters

01 Introduction to AI and Law
02 AI & Law: Autonomous Legal Reasoning
03 AI & Law: Robo-Lawyer Hyperbole
04 AI & Law: Legal Singularity
05 AI & Law: Legal Micro-Directives
06 AI & Law: Legal Argumentation
07 AI & Law: Principles of Justice
08 AI & Law: Reengineering The Law
09 AI & Law: Legal Sentimentality
10 AI & Law: Three Tiers Of Law
11 AI & Law: Turing Test
12 AI & Law: Next Era Of The Law
13 AI & Law: Pure Logic Insufficiency
14 AI & Law: Legal Simplification
15 AI & Law: Dualism With Morality
16 AI & Law: Legal Definitions Of AI
17 AI & Law: Growth In Laws
18 AI & Law: Legal Deserts
19 AI & Law: Open Records
20 AI & Law: OpenAI GPT-3
21 AI & Law: Legal Judgment Prediction
22 AI & Law: Legal Doctrines
23 AI & Law: Tech-Hype Curves
24 AI & Law: LegalTech Startups
25 AI & Law: LegalTech Product Ideas

Appendix A: Teaching with this Material & Bibliography
Appendix B: Supplemental Figures and Charts
About the Author

Available on Amazon and via other online book sellers

Companion Book By Dr. Lance Eliot

"Incisive Research On AI And Law"

ISBN 978-1-73630311-5

Chapters

01 Introduction to AI and Law

02 Framework for Autonomous AI Legal Reasoning

03 AI Turing Test and the Practice of Law

04 Dualism of Moral Agency and AI Legal Reasoning

05 Unauthorized Practice of Law (UPL) and AI

06 Multidimensionality of AI Legal Singularity

07 Principles of Justice and AI Legal Reasoning

08 AI-Enabled Legal Micro-Directives

09 AI Legal Sentiment Analysis and Opinion Mining

10 Anticipating the Fourth Era of the Law

11 Legal Judgment Prediction (LJP) and AI

12 AI and Legal Argumentation

Appendix A: Teaching with this Material

Appendix B: Supplemental Figures and Charts

About the Author

Available on Amazon and via other online book sellers

Companion Book By Dr. Lance Eliot

"Ingenious Essays On AI And Law"

ISBN 978-1-73630312-2

Chapters

01 Introduction to AI and Law
02 AI & Law: Wittgenstein Rules Paradox
03 AI & Law: Deskilling of Human Lawyers
04 AI & Law: Bar Exam Interactive Testing
05 AI & Law: AI-Based Adjudication Dispassionate
06 AI & Law: BigLaw
07 AI & Law: Canons of Contradiction
08 AI & Law: Paperclip Maximizer Qualms
09 AI & Law: Questions of Effective AI Counsel
10 AI & Law: Multijurisdictional Lawyering
11 AI & Law: Digital Twin of the Constitution
12 AI & Law: Antitrust and AI (AAI)
13 AI & Law: AI Arbitrator Impartiality Issues
14 AI & Law: Think Fast and Think Slow
15 AI & Law: Legal Personhood
16 AI & Law: Lower Courts and AI Judges
17 AI & Law: Representational Conflicts
18 AI & Law: Overzealous Lawyering
19 AI & Law: Hybrid Neuro-Symbolic AI
20 AI & Law: Law Schools
21 AI & Law: Chicken Or The Egg
22 AI & Law: Legal Jargon
23 AI & Law: Legal Chess Playing
24 AI & Law: Setting the Bar on Proficiency
25 AI & Law: Repeatedly Trying Is Sane
Appendix A: Teaching with this Material & Bibliography
Appendix B: Supplemental Figures and Charts
About the Author

Available on Amazon and via other online book seller

Companion Book By Dr. Lance Eliot

"Compelling Essays On AI And Law"

ISBN 978-1-73630313-9

Chapters

01 Introduction to AI and Law
02 AI & Law: Echo Chambers In The Law
03 AI & Law: Role Reversible Judgment
04 AI & Law: When AI Is The Criminal
05 AI & Law: Apologetic AI Legal Troubles
06 AI & Law: Personal Digital Identity
07 AI & Law: Stockpiling Legal Postures
08 AI & Law: Law As Code
09 AI & Law: Lawyers As Coders
10 AI & Law: Agile AI And Law
11 AI & Law: Legal Advice By Nanosecond
12 AI & Law: AI-Based Co-Counsel
13 AI & Law: Deferential Behaviors In Law
14 AI & Law: Slowing AI Wheels Of Justice
15 AI & Law: Dehumanizing Lawyers
16 AI & Law: Gifting Of AI Legal Advice
17 AI & Law: When AI Is Evidentiary
18 AI & Law: Legal Maps
19 AI & Law: Posthumanization
20 AI & Law: AI Law Not Computable
21 AI & Law: Collective Intelligence
22 AI & Law: Limits Of Human Mind
23 AI & Law: Judicial Machine Readability
24 AI & Law: Legal Ecosystem
25 AI & Law: Oxford – Autonomous Levels

Appendix A: Teaching with this Material & Bibliography
Appendix B: Supplemental Figures and Charts
About the Author

Available on Amazon and via other online book sellers

Companion Book By Dr. Lance Eliot

"Topnotch Essays On AI And Law"

ISBN 978-1-73630314-6

Chapters

01 Introduction to AI and Law
02 AI & Law: Explainable AI (XAI)
03 AI & Law: Reversing False Memories
0 AI & Law: Antitrust and AI
05 AI & Law: Legal Aid Services
06 AI & Law: Bring Your Own Algorithm
07 AI & Law: Percolation of the Law
08 AI & Law: Rule of Law
09 AI & Law: British Nationality Act
10 AI & Law: Legal API
11 AI & Law: Ramification of Bad AI
12 AI & Law: Computable Contracts
13 AI & Law: C-Suite Buy-in
14 AI & Law: Standards for LegalTech
15 AI & Law: No Code
16 AI & Law: Human Signs of Dishonesty
17 AI & Law: Soft Law on AI
18 AI & Law: Regulating AI
19 AI & Law: Primer on AI and the Law
Appendix A: Teaching with this Material & Bibliography
Appendix B: Supplemental Figures and Charts
About the Author

Available on Amazon and via other online book sellers

Companion Book By Dr. Lance Eliot

"Trendsetting Essays On AI And Law"

ISBN 978-1-95-738601-0

Chapters

01 Introduction to AI and Law
02 AI & Law: Duty To Inform
03 AI & Law: Experimental Jurisprudence
04 AI & Law: Turtles All The Way
05 AI & Law: Animal Rights For AI
06 AI & Law: Languages Translation Access
07 AI & Law: Legal Proximate Cause
08 AI & Law: Judicial Analytics
09 AI & Law: Judge Breakfast
10 AI & Law: Lower Bound Complexity
11 AI & Law: Judges Gambler Fallacy
12 AI & Law: Legal Reconnaissance
13 AI & Law: Legal Fiction To Punish AI
14 AI & Law: Legal Simplification
15 AI & Law: Dropping The Legal Boom On AI
16 AI & Law: Not AL AI Is Equal
17 AI & Law: Legal Argumentation Uncertainty
18 AI & Law: Legal Volition
19 AI & Law: Shadow Docket
20 AI & Law: Legal Reductio
21 AI & Law: Non-Contradictions Resolute
22 AI & Law: Slipper Legal Slopes
23 AI & Law: Unintended Consequences
24 AI & Law: Creative Legal Thinking
25 AI & Law: Thinking Outside The Legal Box
Appendix A: Teaching with this Material & Bibliography
Appendix B: Supplemental Figures and Charts
About the Author

Available on Amazon and via other online book sellers

Companion Book By Dr. Lance Eliot

"Pioneering Essays On AI And Law"

ISBN 978-1-95-738602-7

Chapters

1 Introduction to AI and Law
2 AI & Law: Order Taking Associates
3 AI & Law: Lawyer Conformity
4 AI & Law: Law Firm Rankings
5 AI & Law: Pounding The Legal Table
6 AI & Law: Believing AI Exceptionalism
7 AI & Law: Liquescent Law
8 AI & Law: Precrime Detection
9 AI & Law: Digisprudence
10 AI & Law: Catala Legal Coding
11 AI & Law: Thinking Like A Lawyer
12 AI & Law: Legal Engineers
13 AI & Law: Circular Legal Reasoning
14 AI & Law: Gluing NLP Benchmark
15 AI & Law: Quantum Computational Law
16 AI & Law: Computational Legalism
17 AI & Law: AI You Need To Know
18 AI & Law: Sustainable Legal Informatics
19 AI & Law: Shortcomings Of The AI Act
20 AI & Law: Aged Out AI Predictions
21 AI & Law: Lawyer Reputation
22 AI & Law: AI Judging Judges
23 AI & Law: Online AI Law Courses
24 AI & Law: Overfitting Machine Learning
25 AI & Law: Wet And Dry Code

Appendix A: Teaching with this Material & Bibliography
Appendix B: Supplemental Figures and Charts
About the Author

Available on Amazon and via other online book sellers

Companion Book By Dr. Lance Eliot

"Trailblazing Essays On AI And Law"

ISBN 978-1-95-738603-4

Chapters

01 Introduction to AI and Law
02 AI & Law: Good Old Fashioned AI (GOFAI)
03 AI & Law: Retrospective Learning
04 AI & Law: AI Homogeneous Issues
05 AI & Law: AI As Techno-Regulator
06 AI & Law: Law Design For AI Design
07 AI & Law: Adversarial Precepts
08 AI & Law: Overturned Rulings
09 AI & Law: Dissenting Opinions
10 AI & Law: One-Shot Learning
11 AI & Law: Legal Cases Topological Maps
12 AI & Law: Unit Of Analysis
13 AI & Law: Legislative Facts
14 AI & Law: Law Smells Are Useful
15 AI & Law: Cross-Jurisdictional Law
16 AI & Law: Legal Knowledge Graphs
17 AI & Law: Legal Ontology Patterns
18 AI & Law: Extra-Legal Knowledge
19 AI & Law: Human Lawyers Ahead
20 AI & Law: AI-Completeness
21 AI & Law: Forensic AI Techno-Babble
22 AI & Law: No Vehicles In The Park
23 AI & Law: AI Robo-Jurors
24 AI & Law: Trifecta Of AI Law Roles
25 AI & Law: Judging AI Judges

Appendix A: Teaching with this Material & Bibliography
Appendix B: Supplemental Figures and Charts
About the Author

Available on Amazon and via other online book sellers

ADDENDUM

Thanks for reading this book and I hope you will continue your interest in the field of AI & Law

---

For my free podcasts about AI & Law:

https://ai-law.libsyn.com/website

Those podcasts are also available on Spotify, iTunes, etc.

For the latest on AI & Law see my website:

www.ai-law.legal

To follow me on Twitter:

https://twitter.com/LanceEliot

For my in-depth book on AI & Law:

AI And Legal Reasoning Essentials

www.amazon.com/gp/product/1734601655/

Made in the USA
Monee, IL
05 November 2026

67808613R00125